D1236737

Commitment
and
Healing

Also by the author

Being Homosexual: Gay Men and Their Development

Becoming Gay: The Journey to Self-Acceptance

Commitment and Healing

Gay Men and the Need for Romantic Love

Richard A. Isay, M.D.

John Wiley & Sons, Inc.

Published by John Wiley & Sons, Inc., Hoboken, New Jersey
Published simultaneously in Canada

Design and composition by Navta Associates, Inc.

For general information about our other products and services, please contact our Customer Care Department within the United States at (800) 762-2974, outside the United States at (317) 572-3993 or fax (317) 572-4002.

Wiley also publishes its books in a variety of electronic formats. Some content that appears in print may not be available in electronic books. For more information about Wiley products, visit our web site at www.wiley.com.

Library of Congress Cataloging-in-Publication Data:

Isay, Richard A.
  Commitment and healing : gay men and the need for romantic love / Richard Isay.
      p. cm.
  Includes bibliographical references and index.
  ISBN-13 978-0-471-74049-0 (cloth)
  ISBN-10 0-471-74049-7 (cloth)
1. Gay men—Psychology. 2. Gay men—Mental health. 3. Commitment (Psychology) 4. Love. 5. Interpersonal relations. I. Title.
HQ76.I69 2006
306.76'62—dc22   2005031919

Printed in the United States of America

10 9 8 7 6 5 4 3 2 1

For Gordon Harrell

Contents

Acknowledgments

I have presented parts of this book in their early development at an annual meeting of the American Psychiatric Association (New York, May 2004); Grand Rounds, Department of Psychiatry, Weill Cornell Medical College (New York, December 2003); George Washington University Medical College, as visiting professor and Daniel Prager Lecturer (Washington, D.C., April 2001); Karen Horney Psychoanalytic Institute and Center (New York, January 2001); Grand Rounds, Department of Psychiatry, Lenox Hill Hospital (New York, October 2000); the Department of Psychiatry and Behavioral Medicine, The Norwegian University of Science and Technnology, as visiting professor (Trondheim, Norway; May 2000); and the Section of Psychiatry of the Royal Society of Medicine and at a meeting of the British Association of Psychotherapists (both in London, October 1997).

Tom Miller at John Wiley & Sons liked and accepted this manuscript. He and a terrific staff guided the book through production. My typist, Elizabeth Parella, has been conscientious in returning drafts promptly, helping to keep me on schedule. Fred Morris of the Jed Mattes Agency has supported this book from the time he enthusiastically read an early draft. I am grateful for his unflagging encouragement.

Douglas Heath, my teacher and friend, Professor Emeritus of Psychology at Haverford College, introduced me as an undergraduate to many of the concepts of human development, psychoanalytic psychology, and psychotherapy that have continued to engage and excite me throughout my professional career.

My sons, David and Joshua, have always been supportive and loving, and are a source of great pride. Gordon Harrell, my partner, provided valuable editorial advice with his usual intelligence, incisiveness, and wit. I could have no truer friend, companion, partner, and lover than he.

It is my patients, with their determination, courage, and willingness to confront themselves and to speak with me about their anxieties, fears, passions, and hopes, who have made this book possible. I am grateful to each of them.

Prologue

T his book is about the importance of romantic love for gay men and the difficulty many have in finding or sustaining it. A loving relationship over time can transform anyone's life. The sustained devotion of one person is especially important to gay men who have been rejected or misunderstood by either or both parents in childhood and then by their peers during adolescence. As adults, they usually discover that their capacity to experience or express need is now inhibited and their ability to accept another's love becomes more difficult with every passing year.

Many of these men—mistrusting, fearful, or even unaware of their need for love—have sought happiness without intimacy or intimacy without commitment until midlife. Then a sense of emptiness or aloneness usually convinces them that an intimate and committed relationship combining sexual passion and deep friendship over many years stands the best chance of providing the happiness that has thus far eluded them. By this time, however, most have grown used to the readily available pleasures that they have found can obviate their need for the love of one other person: random sex or brief affairs combined with friendships, work, tasteful surroundings, and sometimes alcohol or other recreational drugs. Others never see the value of love and will not put forth the effort to initiate a relationship or maintain the vulnerability and the dependence that sustain intimacy and keep it interesting and exciting.

Many gay men hope that the legal recognition of same-sex marriage will solve their problems with forming or sustaining intimate relationships. Adopting children or committing to a marriage or a civil union will give some gay men the incentive to maintain these bonds. However, forming a union will not circumvent those difficulties with intimate relationships that originated during childhood and that cause many gay men to mistrust love.

I hope that this book will function like a good therapeutic encounter, resonating with the reader's experience and helping him to understand how the coping mechanisms he used as a child to deal with an irregular love that did not take his needs into account are no longer useful and now contribute to his inability to fall in love or, more commonly, to stay in love.

Those who read this book looking for easy solutions to their difficulties with romantic love will, I fear, be disappointed. Like every human endeavor of value, love requires effort and perseverance to acquire and maintain. The sooner a person learns to value love, the sooner he will work to nourish and sustain it and the more practiced he will become in the art of loving. I hope that through this book, readers will begin discover that they are worth the effort love demands—and that love is worth the effort it demands.

I

The Problem of Romantic Love

It is hard to admit that one was without love in the past. And yet—love would not be the moving, the gripping, the searing experience that it is if the moved, gripped, seared soul were not conscious of the fact that up to this moment it had not been moved nor gripped.
—*Franz Rosenzweig*

Most of my gay patients over the last thirty years have told me about their problems with love. Some have difficulty falling in love, and staying in love is even harder. These may not be the main reasons they seek help, but sooner or later most want to discuss love in their treatment. This book is about the difficulty many gay men have loving and being loved and how I have tried to help them.

I do not limit the concept of romantic love to romance or simply to sexual desire or the rhapsodic experience of falling in love, but I also include the enduring experience of staying in love. Romantic love is based on sexual passion, and this passion is of primary importance early in all relationships of romantic love. The nature and the degree of one's sexual desire, however, will change over time. As romantic love is altered by familiarity and by care and concern for the well-being of another person, it becomes less selfish and more about his needs, less an expression of high-pitched excitement and more about closeness. Committed relationships of romantic love are motivated by the desire for happiness.

Long-term loving relationships are difficult for anyone. Montaigne was convinced that marriage and romantic love were incompatible, and Bertrand Russell doubted they could be reconciled. Freud also wrote about the difficulty of maintaining passion in marital relationships and held that there was always a tension between sexuality and love. Sexual passion was, to Freud, unbridled id suffused with aggression, while love demanded tenderness and affection, warmth and altruism. According to Freud, to achieve love in a relationship, the sexual instincts have to be sublimated. It is not healthy to separate sex and love, he maintains when discussing the whore-madonna complex, and we spend much of our adult life trying to bring love and sex together.

Freud was pessimistic about civilized man ever being truly able to express his sexuality free of inhibition. This was not all bad, though, because sublimated sexual feelings were an enormous source of creativity, and sexual feelings that were "inhibited in their aims . . . are especially adapted to create permanent ties."

Although heterosexuals have difficulty maintaining relationships, committed relationships between gay men are even more difficult to sustain. I am convinced that if these relationships were better, many gay men would have happier and more fulfilling lives.

Gay men and lesbians should have the same legal, financial, and social protections of their committed relationships that heterosexuals do. They should not only be permitted to marry—they should be encouraged to do so. Marriage gives two people who are striving to remain together the sense that their relationship has a special, extraordinary significance. It is a familiar structure within which they can experience and express their love and regard for one another and make the day-to-day accommodations and compromises that all intimate relationships demand. The absence of this structure and of the incentives and the social endorsement for committed relationships contributes to the experience of many gay couples that their relationships are second best. As a result, they make less of an effort to nurture these relationships.

The lack of the right to marry and of the privileges of a socially sanctioned marriage and even the customary absence of children in gay relationships are not the main reasons that most of these relationships do not endure. A more crucial reason is that many gay men lack self-love, which makes it difficult and often impossible to give and accept love over any significant period of time.

True self-love derives from a child having felt loved, accepted, and appreciated. Parental love gives someone the confidence that he or she deserves to be loved and inclines that person to provide regard, support, and affirmation to another, which then encourages love. Those who do not value themselves and who do not believe they are lovable are inclined to be selfish, demanding, mean, or critical in their intimate relationships as a way of discouraging their partners' love. And if a partner, out of love or concern, can disregard the way he is being treated and can make an effort to respond lovingly, his love will usually be rebuffed. Those who lack self-love are convinced that another's love, sooner or later, will turn into the familiar and expected rejection that they believe they deserve.

I've observed that the manner in which homosexual boys are raised and treated by their parents—who are usually uneducated about and unempathic to their children's particular needs—is the main reason most gay men have not developed the love of self that enables them to trust another's love. Some have difficulty falling in love and others find that they are incapable of relying and depending on one other person for an extended period of time. This renders them unable or unwilling to make the commitment that is indispensable for an enduring love.

All men raised in our macho society are acculturated to be independent. As adults, heterosexual men and gay men alike feel encumbered if they must depend on another person, and both make unconscious choices, because of anxiety about their dependency, that may destabilize their intimate relationships. Yet two gay men in a relationship, undeterred by a woman's tolerance for or fostering of a partner's dependence, will often inadvertently but sometimes explicitly encourage each other to have sex outside of the relationship and to make vocational choices that entail long periods of time apart. Extra-relationship sex, preoccupation with one's vocation, and long periods of time apart from one another diffuse unwanted dependence and ultimately undermine both partners' trust in and love for each other, as well as undermine the stability of the relationship.

Our society's continuing prejudice against the expression of homosexual love certainly contributes to the difficulty adult gay men have falling in love or sustaining their relationships over time. Earlier, as adolescents, their fear of rejection may have made it problematic to be openly gay and then difficult to find gay peers for friendships and for romantic and sexual encounters. Gay adolescents still usually hide their sexual orientation, which makes it impossible for them to experiment with and then learn an appropriate courting behavior. This may also result in unavailable straight boys being the exclusive object of a gay adolescent's sexual fantasy, leading to powerful, unrequited, humiliating crushes and often to the rejection that causes further mistrust of relationships.

Many social conservatives base their opposition to same-sex marriage and civil unions on disputed or ambiguous biblical injunctions, on church history, or on the grounds that it would weaken traditional marriage. Others have an apocalyptic vision, fearing it will lead to the "mainstreaming of dysfunction" and to social disintegration. Some gay men are also afraid to normalize their relationships, believing that in doing so, they will be confined by a social acceptance that will deprive them of the freedom to determine the structure of their relationships for themselves.

Because of what I have learned from my patients about their difficulties in forming and sustaining relationships and what I have heard from and observed of friends and acquaintances, I am not confident that this freedom and the sexual openness of gay relationships make these relationships better than heterosexual relationships or a model for relationships in general. Gay men render a valuable service to society with their relative lack of violence, their sensitivity to other minorities, their high rate of volunteerism, and their artistic, civic, and financial contributions. Yet promoting a new sexual democracy or making vocational and other decisions that do not consider the needs of one's partner or of the relationship are more often than not a rationalization for how many gay men deal with their unwelcome needs, lack of self-love, and mistrust of another person's love. Respect for your partner's right to do what he wants in the moment may be democratic in the sense that you don't impose your will on him, but it is often not respectful of the relationship or of both of your long-term needs. Allowing this freedom may eclipse a sense of obligation and duty to each other and may hinder the capacity to make those sacrifices and compromises that are necessary to nourish one another's love.

When self-esteem has been sufficiently injured, and therefore one does not believe that he is lovable or that he deserves to be happy, he may not be able to make the effort or find the courage to deal with normal anxieties and fears that arise in response to everyday challenges. Striving for personal happiness and self-satisfaction is then deemed justifiable only in times of extreme danger or personal crisis. Partly for this reason, at the height of the AIDS epidemic and before there were available treatments, gay men seemed to be more courageous and self-disciplined than they are now; they seemed to demonstrate greater loyalty to one another, to bond more readily in close friendships, and to be more interested in pursuing and sustaining committed romantic relationships. Now that a variety of treatments are available for HIV and AIDS, young gay men, as well as gay men in their thirties and forties, are again pursuing the pleasures of unprotected anonymous sex.

This increased interest in risky sexual activity has been facilitated by easy Internet hook-ups and by the use of crystal methamphetamine, which temporarily bolsters self-confidence and libido while lowering sexual inhibitions. Yet the fact that risky sexual behavior is again rising also suggests that many gay men believe that they do not deserve to be well and happy. They often rationalize their conviction by saying that the fun is worth the risk. Many of these same men also believe that long-term, committed relationships involve too much work. Love requires the belief that one is worth the effort that is necessary to find it and also requires the courage and the self-discipline necessary to sustain it.

Although my observations about gay men's difficulties with intimate, romantic-love relationships are based on a sample of patients, I do not view the men I see in my office as having more problems than those I know outside of my office. They are distinguished from the population as a whole not because they are more disturbed, but because they are more inclined to seek psychological understanding of whatever problems they have, and they possess the intellectual and financial resources, as well as the motivation and the curiosity, to do so.

Most of my patients live in or around New York City. Large metropolitan areas offer more readily accessible alternatives to the love of one other person than do smaller urban or rural areas. A large, supportive gay community, friendships with other gay men, the availability of sex, as well as all the other entertainments and diversions of the city, may make a relationship seem less necessary for personal happiness than it does to people living in a rural area. Outside of metropolitan areas, gay men might be inclined to put forth more effort to make their relationships viable, overcoming by dint of necessity whatever mistrust of love they may have. Although my patient population may not, in this way, be representative, I believe that my observations reflect the difficulties most gay men experience in their relationships.

The philosopher Irving Singer has written that "No one kind of love will satisfy all our needs on all occasions." I know, for example, how important the love of friends is to many gay men, that friends supply the supportive and understanding community of peers many lacked while growing up. Yet I am also convinced that a relationship of romantic love combining deep friendship and passion, in which one loves and feels loved by one other person over many years, is the most effective way to provide the sense of self-worth that can compensate for injuries sustained in childhood and adolescence. Nor, it seems to me, does any other human endeavor provide the same degree of personal happiness as this relationship, which enhances not only your value but your appreciation of others and the pleasure and the beauty one experiences in the world. For many gay men, especially those who are not religious and those who do not have children, loving and being loved in a long-lasting relationship usually gives their lives transcendent significance.

As Plato wrote, "In the business of acquiring immortality, it would be hard for human nature to find a better partner than love."

2

Why Is It Difficult to Need Love?

> If a person isn't aware of a lack, he can't desire the thing he isn't aware of lacking.
> —*Plato*

G ay men who find it difficult to love or be loved usually tell me that they want an intimate relationship or believe they should have one but add that they do not need one to be happy. Some feel humiliated or embarrassed by their need for love; a few are no longer even able to experience it. Experiencing need for another person's love is necessary for both falling in love and staying in love. Though a man may not be aware of this need when he falls in love, he must become aware of it if he is going to make the commitment necessary for staying in love.

The need for love is biological. Because of the rapid growth of the human infant's brain, he has an early birth relative to that of other mammals. This premature birth results in a prolonged period of helplessness and dependence on his parents for survival.

The human brain is most impressionable during the first few years of life. During this time, it encodes what love feels like in terms of how well one's needs are being satisfied and the touch, the vocal tones, the facial expressions, and the behaviors through which these are satisfied. In these years, the child learns what he must do to elicit the love and care he needs. The interplay between a child's ability to signal his needs and the caregiver's response to them provides the model for our loving and being loved as adults.

I am not suggesting that an adult's need for love is the same as an infant's or a child's. Childhood involves a perpetual tension between depending on caregivers and separating from them. Parents must be good enough to impart sufficient comfort and security to their child to enable him to take the literal and figurative steps that are necessary to become an individual. In the process, the nature of his needs differentiates, and the number of people he needs naturally expands from his parents to others. The methods he can use to get love and attention become increasingly nuanced and enhanced as the child emerges from being utterly dependent. Indeed, for an adolescent to develop a crush on another and fall in love, he must be separate enough and secure enough to be confident that he will get something valuable from loving another person. While, paradoxically, the act of falling in love increases the separation and a sense of independence from our parents, throughout our lives we continue to need attachments, in part because they reestablish and re-evoke the imprinted memories of our early relatedness.

The primary reason that any person, gay or straight, has difficulty expressing or experiencing need for another's love is inadequate early parenting. The bond created between a mothering person and his or her child is the child's earliest source of safety and comfort. Disruptions of this attachment in the first year or two are very damaging to an individual's later capacity to form attachments and maintain intimate relationships.

The psychoanalyst René Spitz found that orphaned children and children separated during their first year from mothers who were imprisoned became withdrawn and sickly and sometimes died, even when their physical needs were adequately met. He observed that the lack of human interaction and stimulation at this early age was responsible for these severe disturbances and frequent fatalities. His work was elaborated by the British psychoanalyst John Bowlby, who pointed out how secure early attachments to a mother or a mothering person provide the foundation for future happiness, health, and adult intimate relationships.

When attachments are disrupted in earliest childhood, this has the most profound effect on health and on the capacity to feel trust, which is necessary to attach to another person. Yet rejection by either parent in later childhood also affects the adult's capacity to form intimate relationships. The total diversion of parental attention to a new sibling, the parents' preoccupation with their own needs to the exclusion of their child's, or the emotional exploitation of a child to fulfill his parents' frustrated ambitions are all commonly experienced as rejection. They undermine the child's self-esteem by causing him to believe that his feelings and needs are unimportant and that it would be futile to express them because they will be unfulfilled or met with an unempathic response. If rejection, lack of interest, emotional neglect, or empathic failures have been early, severe, and consistent, a child usually stops asking for what he needs and may soon forget that he needs at all, eventually losing touch with his need for love.

Alan

Alan is a good-looking, muscular forty-six-year-old who started to work with me several years ago when he recognized the difficulty he had in sustaining any loving, romantic attachments. At the time, he told me that he did not really need a relationship because he had good friends and was very involved with his work, but that more and more often at the end of the day, he found it painful to "go home alone."

He was inclined to be attracted and grow attached to men who were emotionally unavailable or not interested in a relationship. Usually, he met them online, and often his sexual partners were either heterosexually married or in relationships with other men. He enjoyed the adventure and the conquest, as well as the sex itself, but whenever he met someone who became interested in him, he grew self-conscious and eager to please. Then he would lose his erection or be unable to ejaculate. If they met more than a few times and a relationship began to develop, he became detached, distant, and bored.

Alan's mother, now in her seventies, had divorced his father when Alan was twelve. She had been depressed throughout his childhood, had seemed overwhelmed by having to care for him and his younger siblings, and was often irritable, critical, and demanding. Her marriage had been unhappy, and she left home to "get herself together" when Alan was nine. Alan's father was the warmer and more reliable parent, but he was also unhappy in the marriage and had difficulty coping with the demands of family and work. The year after Alan's mother returned home, his parents separated permanently, and his father soon remarried. Alan wanted to live with his siblings, his father and his father's new wife, but, as the oldest of the children, he had to stay with his mother because his stepmother was unable to care for all of the children in her new family.

Alan had learned that to get whatever little love and attention was available, he had to be a good boy and should not trouble his parents or express anger and frustration when his needs went unmet or unnoticed. At an early age, he lost touch with his need for love and became determined to use his considerable intelligence and talent to survive without relying or depending on any one person. This determination was reinforced in high school when he developed a close relationship with a greatly admired married teacher who seduced him. Although he had never had sex before, Alan was reasonably comfortable at the time with his same-sex attraction and desire, but he felt betrayed and would not have sex again until his late twenties.

Not long after he started to work with me, Alan became involved with a man who was preoccupied with his work as well as with a previous lover. Alan was attracted to the man's powerful physical appearance, to his domineering nature, and to a familiar emotional indifference that Alan unconsciously experienced as part of any intimate relationship. Sex was hot throughout their two-year relationship, but if his lover had been more available, Alan would have grown bored and emotionally distant. Sooner or later, he would have had difficulty ejaculating due to the unconscious anger that would be provoked by love that he longed for but deeply mistrusted.

·   ·   ·

Alan had childhood interests that were not characteristic of typical straight boys—he never liked rough team sports, preferred playing with girls rather than with boys, and from an early age was interested in dressing up in costumes, dancing, and the dramatic arts. Unlike many homosexual boys, his difficulty with loving attachments did not initially derive from such gender atypicality but from never having experienced a reliable love, due to his mother's emotional limitations and his father's need to establish a new family.

The fathers of most homosexual boys are often indifferent, critical, or outright rejecting of them simply because they are not like regular boys. They have one or more characteristics that are more often associated with girls than with boys. The most frequently observed gender-variant trait is a lack of interest in rough-and-tumble play. Other traits, such as a preference for playing with girls rather than with other boys and being more emotionally expressive than other boys, are also common. Some like to play with dolls, and a few like to try on their mother's or sister's clothes. Each of my patients has recalled that he felt closely bound to his mother because he had more in common with her than with his father. Although not all gay men have these traits as children, most recall having had at least some of them.

The typical homosexual boy is considered a sissy in childhood and early adolescence, even though many of his feminine characteristics vanish during adolescence because of biological influences and his determination to conform to peer and social expectations of maleness. However, pressure to behave more like a typical boy begins long before adolescence, at the age of five or six, when his father, and sometimes his mother as well, starts to admonish him to suppress or change his feminine behavior. His parents are biased by cultural standards of maleness and are usually motivated to get their boy to "stop acting like a girl" because they fear that he will be ostracized by other boys at school and by their concern that his atypicality will reflect poorly on their parenting. Unfortunately, most parents do not give much thought to how these admonitions adversely affect their child's self-esteem.

By the time a homosexual boy is eight or nine, either or both parents may sense that this boy has an erotic interest in his father, in other adult males, or in other boys, even if most homosexual boys are themselves not aware of their same-sex attraction until early adolescence or even later. This early manifestation of same-sex desire may further prompt the emotional withdrawal or outright rejection of both parents but most frequently the father's. Many homosexual boys begin to believe that there is something wrong with them because of how their parents react to their differences from other boys, and they start to mistrust any affection or love that others express for them.

In early childhood, homosexual boys are usually expressive and display their enthusiasm, excitement, and disappointment readily. Parents tend to find this emotional expressiveness girlish and admonish them to be more like regular boys. As a result, some boys stop expressing not only their obvious exuberance but other emotions as well, such as crying, anger, or despair when their needs are not being met. After years of suppressing these affects, many boys and men, on that basis alone, lose touch with the frustrated needs that had originally prompted their emotions.

Andrew

As a boy, Andrew did not like rough sports, he enjoyed playing with girls more than with boys, and he carried his doll around with him. He often followed his mother on her household chores, and, when alone, he took out a broom or a vacuum cleaner and sang and danced, excited because these activities reminded him of her. When he started first grade, both of his parents told him to stop being a sissy. He put his doll away and stopped following his mother on her chores; he also stopped displaying excitement and enthusiasm, and he refused to express anger or to cry when he was unhappy.

I first saw Andrew when he was thirty-five because he wanted an intimate, romantic relationship, which he now feared was beyond his reach. He enjoyed sex and was physically attracted to many types of men, but he was unable to fall in love. He was attractive and intelligent and other men often initially desired him, but they soon lost interest because they found him unfeeling.

Andrew spoke with little affect, even when recalling painful memories—a reflection of the habitual and unconscious control he now exerted over expressing his emotions. Like many gay adults, he craved sexual attention. He worked out regularly to get this attention and to feel and appear more masculine. He found it more difficult to need another person than to be the object of another's sexual desire. He was now embarrassed by his need for love, which made him feel dependent and feminine.

·   ·   ·

A close bond usually forms between a homosexual boy and his mother because of their many shared traits and interests. This bond, however, may make it difficult to separate from her, causing many gay men to fear separation or abandonment and contributing to their concern about needing another person in any intimate, romantic relationship. The mother of a homosexual boy often feels closer to him than to her other boys since he is more like her than they are, and she may communicate her need for him, making the boy's separation from her difficult or impossible. Sometimes a gay adult will not give into his need for another man's love, in order to avoid the anxiety that his mother's closeness and need have imposed on him and to maintain the loyalty to her that she has implicitly demanded.

Jonathan

Jonathan, like Andrew, played with dolls and enjoyed playing with girls more than with other boys. He liked being close to his mother during the day and particularly enjoyed helping her cook. His father had been a high school athlete and could not accept Jonathan's lack of interest in aggressive play. His mother, on the other hand, appreciated Jonathan's gentleness, sweetness, kindness, and artistic inclination, but her unhappy marriage and difficult childhood with a depressed mother had caused her to exploit her attachment to Jonathan and his bond to her. She often told him that he was such a source of comfort, love, and companionship that he felt guilty when he left her to go to kindergarten. He would not separate from her and refused to let his mother leave the classroom. In the privacy of his room at home, he started to spin while holding his mother's scarf over his head, attempting to discharge his anxiety about their separation.

As a young man in his twenties, Jonathan told me how hard he has found it to stay in love. He commented that he lost interest whenever he had to commit to a man because he feared the loss of freedom that any intimate relationship demanded. He always enjoyed anonymous sexual encounters whenever he felt too close to another man: they provided a temporary respite from the sense of confinement that came from needing the love of one other person, just as he had felt confined by his need for his mother and her need for him.

Robert

Robert was thirty-seven when he first came to see me because he had discovered that he could not tolerate dating a man for more than a few nights. He wanted a relationship but found his need for another person embarrassing and uncomfortable. Like Jonathan, he was still burdened by his close relationship to his mother.

He was the youngest of three and his mother's favorite. His father had died in an accident when Robert was five, and his mother had encouraged him to compensate for this loss by remaining close to her and by being the "kind of man his father had been." To please her, Robert had dated girls throughout his adolescence, though he was aware by age thirteen or fourteen of his desire for other boys and men. He did not have sex with men until he went away to college, when it was anonymous or with men who were unavailable. He had recognized even then that he did not want a close relationship because it would disappoint his mother.

When he was thirty-two, he came out to his mother, who became distressed. She rebuked him by saying that his father would be disappointed if he were alive and she beseeched Robert to keep this secret from his father's family. After that, Robert continued to have anonymous sex and many gay friends, a combination of relationships that he found more comfortable than an intimate attachment, which would call his mother's further attention to his homosexuality and threaten the close relationship he continued to have with her.

Because many homosexual boys are not accepted for who they are, by the time they reach adolescence they feel insecure and uncomfortable with themselves and in their interactions with peers. The greater clarity of their same-sex fantasies, an increasing awareness of their desire, and their frustrated attraction to heterosexual peers cause only further fear of rejection. Some adapt to this fear by growing excessively concerned about others' opinions and becoming compliant joiners, shifting alliances and opinions according to what they believe others expect. A few grow defensively but fiercely independent of peer approval. By age fifteen or sixteen, many homosexual boys have considerable unconscious resentment about their parents' lack of acceptance and understanding, but they are usually aware only of anger about being rejected by their peers. Many are, by then, embarrassed by their frustrated need for love, and some, even as adolescents, are unable to experience the need that is necessary for both loving and being loved.

Relying on Alternative Pleasures

Gay men who seek help because they cannot form or sustain a relationship are usually in their late thirties or early forties. By that time, most of them have learned to compensate for their lack of an intimate, loving relationship by seeking satisfaction in the pleasures of sexual encounters, the love of friends or extended family, and their work.

In his elegant book *The Elusive Embrace*, Daniel Mendelsohn writes of the advantage of having made a "family" for himself because he cannot get the love he needs from other gay men, whom he finds unreliable, "too vain, too false, too beauty-oriented." He divides himself between "Chelsea, a culture of play" and his friend Rose and her son Nicholas. He loves them both deeply and they love him; from them, he gets the love and the identity that he believes the "culture-damaged boys" cannot provide.

"You may live in two places. . . . In one of these places you may love your boys, your men who are boys, yearn for and sometimes possess their bodies, while in the other you may spend your time caring for a small child, a little boy, while living there with his mother, with a woman."

A variation on this theme of requiring a "family" in lieu of needing the love of another man is found in homosexual men who marry women. They often derive enough emotional security and comfort in a close emotional bond with a spouse and children that for many years they do not desire a relationship with another man. They may have anonymous sex or brief affairs but, until their forties, most do not want to give up their perceived respectability for a relationship that still carries disapprobation. And while they may long for an intimate relationship with another man, they are unable to leave their marriages because of the emotional connection to their spouses and children.

This dilemma was poignantly captured in a letter written to me several years ago by a man in his late forties who had been married for more than twenty years:

> It has been some years since my last sexual experience with a man, but that hasn't reduced the longing to be with one, to be held closely, and to be told that he loves me. I have two (straight) friends who I am close to, who hug me often and express that they love me, but I could never express to them what I truly feel and constantly keep on my guard with them. It's hard to explain the ache that one has and the longing to be close to another man.
>
> I know that I did not pursue the orientation that I have and know that I have always been as I am now. I know that it becomes more difficult to live in the lonely shell that I do now, but I can see no way out of it.

Andrew Sullivan compares romantic love unfavorably to friendship in his book *Love Undetectable*: "In almost every regard, friendship delivers what love promises but fails to provide. . . . Where love is swift, for example, friendship is slow. Love comes quickly as the song has it, but friendship ripens with time. If love is at its most perfect in its infancy, friendship is most treasured as the years go by."

Reliance on extended family, a heterosexual spouse, or friends, in concert with random sexual experiences, is not the only means by which gay men attempt to compensate for their need for the love of another man, as well as avoid the hurt and the rejection they learned from their relationships with parents and then with peers in adolescence. Some are gratified by their work in lieu of an intimate relationship with a man, and others seek the comfort of a nonhuman environment such as a home that can be controlled and perfected and that offers, for a time, the sense of warmth and security that they cannot trust another person to provide.

Charles

Charles, a highly intelligent and successful businessman, was unable to sustain an intimate relationship because he inevitably lost interest in the man he was with. Love had little value for him. His parents were barely twenty when he was born. They had abundant needs of their own and little tolerance for the needs of their oldest child. By the time he was five or six, he had begun to suppress the feminine traits and behaviors that displeased his parents. He had learned to please them by being a good boy and by excelling at school but had never learned to rely on love or to experience need for another's love. When he started therapy, Charles was in his early thirties and was preoccupied with work, achievement, and the opinion of colleagues to the exclusion of intimate relationships. He loved the comfort of his apartment, where he entertained friends. He couldn't understand, he told me, the concept of needing love for his happiness, though he could understand the need for money and respect. He felt alone and isolated and wanted a boyfriend because he felt he should have one, but he did not believe he needed an intimate relationship to be happy.

I have seen the love and the gratification some gay men derive from their relationships with heterosexual spouses and children, friends and extended family, their work and their homes. Yet most of these men, who in their twenties or early thirties denied needing a lasting romantic relationship with another man or were too embarrassed by their need to pursue one, begin to long for one in their late thirties or forties. Many discover that sexual encounters and short-term relationships provide only transient pleasure. They appreciate the love of friends but now find that their friends have their own preoccupations, sometimes including partners, and cannot provide the consistent love and attention that they long for. They become increasingly aware of the anxiety and the pain of loneliness and more apprehensive about aging and rejection. They also worry about their mortality and future illness. It is in their forties that most gay men grow to understand that only a lasting loving relationship with another man will provide them with a sense of self-worth and ultimate happiness.

By the time they want a relationship, some gay men find it difficult to undo the adaptations they have made in order to deny their need for the love of one other man: sex with strangers, brief affairs, exclusive reliance on friends, a heterosexual marriage, work, increasing self-absorption, a preoccupation with their looks, the creation of a beautiful and comforting environment that they inhabit alone, or the excessive use of alcohol and recreational drugs. They may by then have discovered that it is hard to develop a capacity for caring, concern, and compassion that will enable them to sustain love and incorporate their passionate erotic desire into an intimate, loving affiliation.

The psychoanalyst Erich Fromm wrote that one must be aware that love is an art and that one must practice this art to become skillful at it. "The mastery of the art must be a matter of ultimate concern: There must be nothing else in the world more important than the art."

3

Love and Sex in Adult Gay Relationships

Yes, sex and love were different items when he
wanted them in one, and yes, having so much sex
made having love impossible. . . . All I see is guys
hurting each other and themselves. . . . And how
to say all this to anyone, when no one is
listening, no one wants to hear?
—*Larry Kramer*

I first met Ben when he was thirty-two. He sought therapy because he and Aaron, his partner of five years, had not had sex for the previous three years. Initially, he had been attracted to Aaron, and sex had been exciting, passionate, and frequent, but when they began to live together after dating for about a year, sex became less frequent and much less exciting. By the end of the third year, they considered each other best friends, but they were no longer having sex. They agreed that it was all right to have sex outside of the relationship because they lacked sexual desire for each other, but these contacts were to be casual, there was to be no emotional connection to any sexual partner, and they would not discuss their contacts with each other. Although Ben described his life as being more stable and happier than ever before, he was now troubled by his increasing alienation from Aaron. They had started to take Ecstasy together from time to time to recapture the warm and loving feelings that had characterized the first two years of their relationship.

Most of the gay men I work with have found it hard to include sexual passion in their loving partnership. After making a commitment, which may take the form of moving in together as Ben and Aaron had done, being convinced that "this is the person I want to spend my life with," making an explicit and formal domestic partnership agreement, or having a marriage ceremony, most gay men find they cannot sustain their attraction and desire. Within the first two or three years, the average "committed" gay couple has begun to look for sexual gratification outside of the relationship, which both partners hope will not interfere with or threaten this primary affiliation. As a result, within five years, very few relationships are sexually exclusive. Whether explicitly or implicitly sanctioned by the couple, sexual encounters that are new and unencumbered by familiarity are found to be more exciting than sex with one's partner, and these encounters usually turn into the preferred and exclusive way of satisfying sexual desire.

Not only gay men, of course, find it difficult to bring sex and love together in a committed relationship and to maintain sexual interest in their partners. Freud, noting the split between passion and affection in committed heterosexual relationships, memorably wrote of his male patients "where they love, they do not desire, and where they desire, they cannot love." He believed that their "psychical impotence" was caused by the arousal of incestuous feelings toward their mothers whenever sexual impulses occurred in intimate, affectionate relationships, but that love and sex should be integrated for a "completely normal attitude in love."

Others have not been as certain as Freud that integrating sex and love is beneficial to a relationship. The sixteenth-century essayist Montaigne had no doubt that sexual desire toward one's spouse was destructive of the relationship between husband and wife and wrote, "I see no marriages that sooner or later are troubled and failed than those that progress by means of beauty and amorous desires. . . . [Marriage] needs more solid and stable foundations and we need to go about it circumspectly. . . . Ebullient ardor is no good for it. . . ." Four centuries later, the philosopher Bertrand Russell saw marriage solely as an institution for raising children, and he opined that sexual passion for one's spouse interfered with this primary obligation.

The prevalence of casual sex outside of committed relationships and the diminished or total absence of sex within them are considered by many gay men to be not only a normal response to being in a couple but to benefit these relationships. McWhirter and Mattison suggest that sex with others helps a relationship by reestablishing the healthy autonomy of the partners. Dennis Altman considers the absence of monogamy to be a way that gay men create "new forms of relationships" in which fidelity is measured in terms of emotional commitment and not simply in "sexual terms": the absence of sexual monogamy should be a model for relationships in which "neither partner is prepared to subordinate his or her interest to the other. . . ." And, more recently, David Nimmons makes a virtue of our "expansive forms of intimacy," writing that we extend the idea of intimacy with our different relationships such as "fuck buddies, communal homes, and three-way loverships and innovative community practices such as the touch and massage networks." It does not appear to be a concern that when such "innovations" and extramarital adventures occur on a regular basis, they are usually destructive to one's primary relationships. While monogamy may not be necessary for maintaining a long-term, emotionally committed relationship, striving for sexual fidelity minimizes occasions for painful jealousy, lying, and evading the truth, all of which do occur even when sex with others is condoned. Honesty may not in every circumstance be the best policy, but dishonesty over time inevitably undermines a person's sense of self-worth, conveys a lack of regard for and to one's partner, and destroys the trust essential to a loving relationship.

Sexual Fidelity

In the animal world, sex is primarily for reproduction, and monogamy is exceedingly rare. Where monogamy has evolved, it appears to have done so because it provides an advantage in raising offspring and in forming the stable pair needed to defend scarce resources from intruders. For humans, of course, sex is more than the means of species propagation; it is an important way to express and receive a variety of pleasures, including tenderness, affection, comfort, and even aggression. Unless we seek others to gratify these biological and psychological needs, we need our partners in order to satisfy them.

When sex is not for species propagation and there are no children, as is still true for most gay couples, one's partner and the relationship itself are likely to be even more necessary for comfort, security, and happiness than they are for heterosexual couples, whose emotional needs are often partly satisfied by or displaced onto their children. For heterosexual couples, it is often not until their children become more independent or leave home that partners grow increasingly reliant upon each other. And then, as so many gay couples do much sooner in their relationships, heterosexual couples may find their partners lacking some essential qualities or may discover that the partners are unable to satisfy their emotional needs. Thus they seek other sources of emotional and sexual gratification, which sometimes leads to the dissolution of marriages.

Striving for sexual fidelity as well as emotional fidelity is particularly difficult for gay men. The nature of male sexuality makes it unnecessary for most men to establish an emotional connection in order to have sexual pleasure, and it is easy to find sexual partners, especially in urban areas. The problem isn't that occasionally "getting off" with someone outside of one's primary relationship is necessarily harmful. It may even add some excitement to a relationship for a time. The problem is that sex with strangers and the adventures that accompany it are so compelling and exciting that sooner or later, random sexual contacts subvert desire for a more-familiar partner.

Sex Outside of Relationships

Anonymous sexual encounters and brief or, more tellingly, long affairs are a way that gay men deal with unwanted need for their partners and anxiety about commitment and intimacy. These encounters also may serve to discharge unconscious anger or to evoke jealousy—both of which are usually better articulated than acted on, out of concern for one's sense of self-worth and respect for one's partner and the relationship. Dennis Altman's view that gay couples have fewer unrealistic illusions about the permanence of their relationships than straight couples do may be correct. Yet it is their expectation of impermanence that prompts some gay men to unwittingly seek instability and promote the very impermanence they fear. This keeps many gay men from making the necessary effort and the sacrifice of momentary pleasure that could enable them to integrate greater sexual passion into their loving relationships and to discover the comfort and the closeness that occur in sex with one's partner. It deprives them of the opportunity to gain more pleasure from their relationship and greater happiness as well.

Depending on another person is usually frightening. It may evoke fear that he will be hurt or abandoned; almost always, dependence makes us feel like children. Most gay men and many straight men deal with the vulnerability that their dependence elicits by seeking excitement outside of their primary relationship, rather than by putting effort into making the vulnerability itself exciting and thereby, as Stephen Mitchell wrote, making the relationship more interesting and dangerous.

It should not be surprising that gay men feel especially uncomfortable with the natural dependence evoked in their intimate relationships. All boys in our culture are raised to believe that dependence is feminine and therefore find it frightening as adults to rely on one another. Yet because typical homosexual boys have more feminine traits than straight boys do and because they have usually been admonished to repudiate these, by the time they are adults many gay men

abhor the remnants of their sissy boyhood and dislike looking and feeling feminine. Some seek sexual diversion to
diminish their dependence and need for their partners, in an
effort to assuage their discomfort with the feminine feelings
that their dependence has evoked.

Unlike a heterosexual boy's erotic feelings for his
mother, the homosexual boy's earliest sexual sensations may,
as I mentioned earlier, be connected to a father who more
often than not finds his boy too different from him for his
comfort, and favors his other children, male and female.
Because many of the peers to whom this boy is attracted in
later childhood and adolescence are heterosexual and therefore rejecting and unattainable, as an adult he may discover
that he is attracted only to men who are familiarly rejecting
or sexually unattainable. In retaliation for his father's earlier
rejection, he may reject anyone who cares about him, finding that person boring or unattractive. Or, by demonstrating
lack of sexual interest in a loving partner, over time he will
turn that partner into one of the familiar uninterested, dep-
recating, rejecting figures from his childhood and adolescence.

Some gay men may be initially attracted to a certain
type of partner because of his perceived masculinity and can
acknowledge that his strong arms or muscularity reminds
them of their fathers or other straight relatives from childhood. After a while, however, as they grow more emotionally attached, the recognition of their attraction to men who
resemble their fathers makes them anxious enough to lose
their sexual interest. They discover that they are much more
excited by men to whom they are not so intimately bonded.
Attraction may be further eroded when they recognize that

their partners have become increasingly dependent on them and therefore seem to be less masculine and more vulnerable to being hurt by any anger or conflict. Many gay men search for sex with strangers, not only because the unfamiliar is more exciting, but because strangers are not dependent, they seem to be more masculine, and they appear invulnerable to retaliatory anger.

Often, a gay man diverts sexual interest from a partner because his dependence makes him feel suffocated; he believes that his freedom is being intruded upon. He becomes anxious because the intimacy is reminiscent of his earlier dependence on a mother who had expected too much or imposed too many demands in order to make herself happy. She often ignored her son's needs and wishes, which led to his conviction that his needs and internal life were unimportant. In his closeness to a partner, no matter how thoughtful, compromising, or caring this partner may be, he experiences himself as being similarly imposed upon and feels helpless to assert either his independence or his own needs.

Gay men have, of course, been acculturated to separate sex and love. There have been social and political gains over the last twenty years, but sexual acts between people of the same gender are still considered abhorrent by most members of our society, and those who openly express their attraction are often the object of contempt and sometimes abuse. Many homosexual adolescents internalize this hatred and, as adults, consider themselves bad or sinful because of their desire. A gay man may therefore desire where he has no love and love where he has no desire because love does not belong with sex that is considered bad or sinful.

Because society has not, as yet, found courting for gay adolescents to be acceptable, for many gay men masturbation to pornography, anonymous encounters in public washrooms, and sex at pornographic movie theaters are still their only sexual outlets. The excitement of having sex with strangers in precarious locations is a learned pleasure that often becomes habitual.

Jealousy

The prevalence of splitting off sex from love in gay male relationships is also an attempt to minimize jealousy. This painful emotion evolved from our primitive need to compete for limited sexual and environmental resources and from the manifest aggression we needed to repulse intruders who threatened these resources. Most likely, jealousy first developed in humans simply to warn of threats to reproductive and food supplies, but later, with the formation of families, it warned when a third person was a threat to a sexual object who was also the source of love and security for oneself and one's offspring.

Jealousy is an emotion that does not always portray threats accurately or realistically; it alerts us to dangers that may be imagined as well as real. When it alerts us to an imagined, unrealistic menace, it is often harmful, provoking a possessiveness that may destroy our relationships. When jealousy is evoked by a real threat, however, it is usually beneficial.

Most gay men in committed relationships will never acknowledge their sexual jealousy. They recognize and

accept jealousy of one another over work, money, possessions, or even the attention of friends and acquaintances, but
they generally disavow the existence of sexual jealousy in
their most intimate relationships. It is partly in order to
deny their sexual jealousy that many reject the notion of
even striving for monogamy; they unrealistically hope that
any agreed-upon outside recreational sexual contacts will
help and not destroy their primary relationships.

A gay philosopher has written, "When one is . . . able to
freely give [one's body] to others, one has no need to own
someone else's body like a prosthetic device or to worry
about what others are doing with their bodies. This is not to
say that one does not run into all of jealousy's vile putrefac-
tion in many a closed, gay male relationship." An early gay
activist wrote, "We should put an end to our embarrassment
about transcending monogamy, for by moving beyond it we
have also transcended the possessiveness and jealousy
adopted from traditional heterosexual relationships." And
McWhirter and Mattison in their study of male couples suggest that the lack of possessiveness and jealousy from
agreed-upon sexual contacts is "the single most important
factor that keeps couples together past the ten year mark."

Coupled gay men expend so much effort denying their
sexual jealousy because intimate, committed relationships
are so essential for their ultimate happiness and sense of
well-being. Jealousy makes them aware of their need for
love and security, which is often humiliating because most
gay men are convinced that their emotional needs will not
be met; if they rely too much on one other person, they will
again be injured or rejected as they were in childhood and
adolescence. Jealousy, like other strong affects, is often

viewed as a sign of being effeminate; experiencing this feeling is repugnant to most gay men. Jealousy, however, may be useful in maintaining our intimate affiliations, and when gay men deny that it exists, they often place their relationships at risk.

Gerald

Gerald, a successful businessman in his midthirties, had been with his lover for about five years. They were initially very attracted to each other, but their attraction waned after they moved in together. They agreed to have recreational sex outside of their relationship, though Gerald did not want to be told of Hal's infidelities, believing that he would be jealous. He sought therapy because the relationship was deteriorating and because he was increasingly furious with Hal—not, he pointedly told me, for Hal's infidelity, but because he missed Hal's companionship.

Gerald had been very competitive with his three-years-younger brother, who was handsome, outgoing, athletic, and adventurous. His brother was strikingly different from Gerald, who was quiet, unathletic, and bonded to his self-involved, depressed mother. His father adored this younger brother, ignoring and sometimes ridiculing Gerald, who then took every opportunity to express his resentment and jealousy by teasing, disparaging, and at times bullying his brother. He felt guilty about his abusiveness—guilt that, as an adult, he attempted to atone for by instigating others to get angry at him and by making self-defeating choices. Gerald saw his partner as being like his comely, handsome, popular, and better-loved younger brother and was aware of being jealous of Hal for his physical attributes and social skills. As a way of denying any humiliation over this jealousy, however, he encouraged Hal to pursue sexual adventures, about which he became more and more resentful.

Because Gerald did not enjoy sex with strangers, he seldom sought outside sexual contacts, but he was increasingly lonely and found himself spending more and more time with friends or at work. Though he eventually told his partner that the relationship was "not working," he continued to deny that he was in any way jealous of Hal's sexual adventures. Although their relationship was, for many reasons, not a good or a happy one, it was, we later discovered, mainly to avoid acknowledging and confronting the pain of his chronic and intense jealousy that Gerald decided to ask Hal to leave.

Many gay men, like Gerald, deny their jealousy because they do not want to experience the humiliation they felt when their fathers rejected them by favoring other siblings. And, as we have seen, during adolescence, many are further humiliated by their attraction to dismissive peers. Unlike heterosexual boys, for whom jealousy is an accepted response to a third party's intrusion on their relationships, homosexual adolescents often find their jealousy shameful because of the sexual arousal that initiated it and because they will be scorned for expressing it. They have learned not to acknowledge jealousy to themselves, to the objects of their unrequited desire, or to intruders.

Inviting another person, usually a stranger, to have sex in a "three-way" is ostensibly to enhance the flagging sexual excitement that partners have for each other. Sometimes three-ways become a favored sexual activity because they often evoke the jealousy that makes one or the other partner feel desired. Yet most gay couples who engage in three-ways do so in the futile attempt to demonstrate that neither partner has any jealousy over the other's outside sexual interests or activities. Three-ways are almost always, sooner or later, harmful to a relationship, prompting one or both partners to feel rejected and often unconsciously angry and vindictive.

Ben and Joseph

Two men in a long-standing relationship were aware of the intense jealousy each had of the other, but they denied their sexual jealousy. The older of the two resented the attention his younger, more attractive partner received from mutual friends as well as strangers; the younger envied the acclaim his partner received from his vocation.

Sex was not satisfying to either man after they moved in together, and they made an unarticulated, implicit agreement that it was all right to have sexual activity outside of their relationship as long as it never came to the other partner's attention. They were convinced that if these adventures were not mentioned, neither partner would become jealous. As sex between them became less frequent over the years, they occasionally invited a third person to have sex with them, always making an effort to include each other in the sexual activity. Yet despite their efforts, it was impossible for both partners to be included at all times, and one or the other always felt excluded and jealous.

It was sometimes the older partner, to the surprise of his younger lover, who became the focus of attention from a third person. As a result, the younger man became painfully aware of his sexual jealousy during these three-ways, but, acting quickly to suppress his jealousy, he diverted his anger through casual sexual adventures of his own. Sensing that they were both sexually preoccupied with other people, but never acknowledging or expressing their jealousy, they became less and less affectionate and more emotionally withdrawn from each other. Their relationship ended after six years.

Robert

Robert, whom I mentioned in chapter 2, had his first sexual contacts with his future lover in a succession of three-ways. These experiences foreshadowed distressing jealousy in the relationship.

He had formed a close bond with his mother, even closer than that of most homosexual boys, due to his father's frequent long absences occasioned by his work. After his father's death in an accident when Robert was five, Robert was resentful and jealous that his mother was distracted by her grief and depression. He worked hard to relieve her unhappiness by being good and charming but inevitably discovered that his efforts were inadequate.

Throughout his adolescence and young adulthood, Robert was well aware that he tended both to be jealous and to evoke jealousy. His one previous extended romantic relationship was in college with a young man who was concurrently involved with a woman; it had been replete with jealousy. His friendships, as well, were often close and tempestuous, marked by his abrupt shifts of attention from one friend to another, provoking jealousy among them.

Robert sought therapy because he recognized that he had difficulty establishing the gratifying long-term romantic relationship that he longed for. After about a year of treatment, he met his future partner Michael at a bar. He invited Michael home, initially unaware that Michael was at the bar with his partner of many years. The three of them then had the first of several three-ways that resulted in Michael and Robert falling in love and caused the dissolution of Michael's long but troubled relationship.

After they moved in together, about a year after meeting, Robert became preoccupied with Michael's sadness over his breakup and was convinced that his love and companionship would not be enough to make Michael happy. It was redolent of the way he had been resentful and guilt-ridden over his mother's depression after his father's death. The guilt he felt from taking Michael away from his lover and securing Michael's love was intensified by a continued close attachment to his mother and the unconscious belief that he was betraying her.

Risk Taking, HIV, and Love

Men are by nature aggressive adventure-seekers and risk-takers. Homosexual boys seem to be generally less physically aggressive than heterosexual boys are, but adult gay men, like heterosexual males, are also risk-takers and adventure-seekers. This may partly account for their quest for different sexual partners. Two men together, unimpeded by a woman's desire for the stability that will benefit the raising of offspring, are more inclined than is a heterosexual couple to seek sexual adventures that may place their health, their partner's health, and their relationship in jeopardy. It is unfortunate for both their relationships and their health that these two traits appear to be gender conforming and not "shifted" in gay men, as many other traits are.

Acquiring HIV and AIDS, however, has also made it possible for some gay men to find love and enter into committed relationships for the first time. In the 1980s and early 1990s, when HIV and AIDS were usually fatal and many gay men believed that their dependency and need were therefore time-limited, several patients whom I treated seemed enabled to love because they had become ill. For each of these men, only the prospect of death made it possible for him to reorder his priorities from pleasurable diversion to a fuller appreciation of the love of one person that might ultimately bring him greater happiness.

David

David came to see me in 1980 because he was depressed, felt isolated, and believed that he would never be able to have an intimate relationship. He told me he had always been depressed. His mother had never expressed warmth or affection; she had loved him, he said, simply because he was talented and smart. Nevertheless, they formed a close bond because they shared mutual interests and his mother needed him as consolation for her unhappy marriage. His father was much warmer than she was, and David longed for his father's affection, but his father preferred David's younger brother, who was more masculine, athletic, and companionable. David was filled with rage at both his parents, rage that he repressed and directed against himself. As a consequence, he placed himself in dangerous situations, especially in seeking sex.

From the time he began to have sex as a third-year college student, he preferred hustlers. Some of them emotionally abused him. On one or two occasions when he was in medical school, his apartment was robbed and he was physically threatened; once his car was stolen. Despite David's financial generosity, these young men inevitably left him, infuriated by David's manipulativeness or sometimes by their increasing dependence on him. These relationships seemed to have recaptured the experience of both his mother's abusiveness and his father's unattainable love. The unreliable nature of his relationships with these young men also enabled David to limit the unwanted reliance, dependence, and need he may have experienced for them.

David hated being homosexual. He thought of himself as sick and repeatedly reminded me that he was perverse. He asked me to help him to have heterosexual sex so that he could give his parents the grandchildren they longed for. He wanted to be heterosexual to win his father's love, a love that was lavished primarily on his heterosexual, outgoing younger brother.

David also hated his body. He believed that his hips, thighs, and buttocks were more like a woman's than a man's. His persistent desire to be dominated and anally penetrated made him feel feminine and it revolted him, reminding him of the ways in which he was like his mother. He avoided associating with other gay men who were effeminate because he believed they called attention to his own femininity.

I had been treating David for about one year when, in June 1981, the Centers for Disease Control (CDC) reported that five previously healthy gay men had developed pneumocystis pneumonia. In July, they reported that Kaposi's sarcoma had been found in twenty-six gay men during the previous thirty months. Within a year, the CDC was suggesting that this illness was sexually transmitted.

I informed David explicitly of the potential dangers of his indiscriminate sexual behavior, telling him what little I knew at that time about the nature of what was then being called GRID (Gay-Related Immune Deficiency), the possible ways it could be transmitted, and the steps he might take to keep from acquiring it. David was in his last year of medical school, but he disavowed having any knowledge of the disease, questioned whether it even existed, and wondered whether my concern was an expression of my homophobia.

He continued to question the validity of my information and my motives for bringing it up. Aside from wondering whether I was homophobic, he believed I was jealous of his sexual prowess. He exhorted me to be more "analytic" and objective and less concerned about his health. My concern evoked a desire in him to be taken care of. This frightened and infuriated him—he experienced me as being like his mother and as having little recognition of how his needs were separate from mine. He was also afraid that when he felt close to me, his rage would either destroy me or drive me away, and, we later learned, his affectionate feelings toward me prompted erotic thoughts that frightened him.

In the fall of 1985, David told me that he was having

diarrhea and night sweats and that he had noticed swollen lymph nodes. He thought he had the flu, treated himself with Tylenol, and refused to see a physician.

Another patient had died a few weeks after David first mentioned his symptoms; several other patients had by then consulted me because of their anxiety about either having AIDS or contracting it. I had one friend and several acquaintances who were sick, and, of course, I also felt it was possible that I could be HIV-positive. My attempt to give David advice was the only way I could try to exert control over the effect this disease was having on my own life.

I suggested that he see one of the growing number of physicians who worked with AIDS patients. He refused, which frustrated and irritated me—reactions he often tried to elicit to make himself feel that I cared about him and was not neglecting him. My irritation also enabled him to maintain some sense of a boundary between us, which he had been unable to experience with his mother.

By now, five years into his therapy, David was more accepting of his homosexuality than he had been at the beginning of treatment. He understood that he had been repulsed by it because he experienced being homosexual and the desire to be close to his father as being like his mother. He also now understood more about the ways he had internalized society's hatred of homosexuals. The progress he had made in dealing with his own homophobia helped him to express his sexuality in less self-destructive and more gratifying ways. And his new understanding and recent good feeling enabled him to feel hopeful about his future.

Three months after first telling me of his night sweats and swollen lymph nodes, David mentioned that he had met a graduate student at a bar near his apartment. They saw each other often during the following weeks, and for the first time David fell in love. They were affectionate and caring of one another, and their relationship grew with surprising rapidity. After a couple of months, they entered into a joint business venture. The following year, Andrew moved into David's apartment.

It was not until six months after meeting Andrew that David finally consulted a physician. This was before the virus had been identified and when the progress of the disease was monitored by the number of T-cells and not by the viral load. On the second visit David was told that his T-cells were very low. The next day he told me how frightened he was and that he was worried about how long he had to live. He then spoke about Andrew: "He never looked so beautiful as he did yesterday. I feel more alive with him than I ever felt before. There aren't words to describe what he means to me. He is a constant source of support. I hope I live long enough to enjoy him." Andrew and David remained together throughout David's illness and until his death three years later. From the time they met, David never again had sex with a hustler, nor did he have an inclination to do so.

David often told me that the relationship made him feel stable and centered, that he no longer yearned for physical comfort from strangers. He recognized how much more receptive he was to being loved than ever before. His fear of dying and what he experienced as the life-giving quality of Andrew's love enabled David for the first time to acknowledge his need for love.

.   .   .

There is tension in any man's life between the quest for security and the thirst for newness, excitement, and adventure. Our early life is spent in adventurous and sometimes frightening separations from parents as we learn the advantages of locomotion and greater independence and then, later, the pleasures that others can offer. Children and even adolescents renew themselves by touching base from time to time with the love, security, and comfort their parents offer, which, if it's good enough, eventually enables them to love other people.

For many gay men to trust that their love will not be betrayed and to appreciate that love is even better at sustaining them in suffering than suffering is at sustaining love, they have to learn to value love and security over the excitement of the new and the unfamiliar. Only the conviction that enduring romantic love offers the best opportunity for ultimate happiness will motivate a gay man—before illness, aging, or fear of dying mandate it—to exercise the self-awareness, self-control, courage, and determination that can subvert his compelling, inherent interest in adventure and the pleasure of the moment for the love and devotion of one other person.

4

Falling in Love

At our first meeting . . . we found ourselves so
captivated, so familiar, so bound to one another,
that from that time nothing was closer to either
than each was to the other. . . . It was some
mysterious quintessence . . . which possessed
itself of my will, and led it to plunge and lose
itself in his. . . . I may truly say *lose*, for it left
us with nothing that was our own, nothing
that was either his or mine.
—*Michel de Montaigne*

F alling in love may be wonderful for some, but for others, it's easier said than done. This passionate attachment may not be necessary to form a loving, committed relationship, and it is far from all that is needed to do so. Falling in love, however, binds one to another person; it often motivates the desire to explore a life together and usually enhances sustained interest in and devotion to one's partner over the years.

Some gay men cannot experience this passion. Each of the gay men I have worked with who has had difficulty falling in love has been unable to detach from his mother. He remains attached to her not because she has been emotionally bountiful, but because she has made it impossible for him to trust that needing another person will get him the love he desires. He usually has the compelling but most often unconscious hope that some day he will get from his mother the love that she never gave but that he continues to long for. Because many gay men have not been given the love they need, they will not turn to human intimacy for their comfort and happiness but rely primarily on their possessions, work, and home, along with some superficial relationships that do not require much need for another person. They eventually discover that they are no longer capable of feeling the fervent desire necessary to fall in love, but they want to be able to do so.

The thrust of physiological development is toward greater and greater independence from our parents, but there is always tension between striving for autonomy and longing to remain attached and be taken care of. To be able to fall in love, we must have been given enough love to believe that it will be forthcoming from another person. We must experience need for the love that has been lost. If we continue to long for love from a mothering parent because we have felt deprived by her (or him), then we usually can not experience enough passionate desire to be able to fall in love.

In the *Symposium*, Plato illustrates the conflict between the wish to stay attached and the need to separate from the mothering parent if one is going to fall in love and rediscover the happiness that has been lost. In an evocative speech by Aristophanes, he portrays the child's original union with his parent as a rounded whole with backs and sides forming a circle. Because Zeus was enraged by the arrogance of humans, he weakens them by separating each circle into two halves. If the child wants to be "grafted together" again to his parent and refuses to search for another, he will die.

It was their very essence that had been split in two, so each half missed its other half and tried to be with it;

they threw their arms around each other in an embrace and longed to be grafted together. As a result, because they refused to do anything without their other halves, they died of starvation and general apathy. If one of a pair died while the other half was left alive, the survivor went in search of another survivor to embrace, and it didn't matter to it whether the half that it fell in with was half of what had originally been a female whole . . . or of a male whole.

Erich Fromm also wrote about this search for lost love and how the awareness of separateness from one's mother arouses a sense of aloneness and need for another: "The deepest need of man, then, is the need to overcome his separateness, to leave the prison of his aloneness. . . . Only to the degree that the child develops his sense of separateness and individuality is the physical presence of the mother not sufficient any more, and does the need to overcome separateness in other ways arise." If one does not eventually feel split from the person who mothers and does not experience longing and need for someone else to provide the love, the comfort, and the security that she offered, one will not be able to fall in love.

It is during the years of prolonged dependence on the mothering parent that we learn about the care and the comfort to expect from relying on another person. If there has been a disruption in this relationship during infancy or childhood from extensive separations, neglect, or, more often, from the caregiver's lack of interest in the child's needs and from his or her inability to be empathic, the boy learns that being dependent on another human being is useless because it does not get him what he needs. He begins to believe that he must not be worth love, attention, or understanding or he would be getting it. Unless there is some dramatic and consistent change in future circumstances that affects his emotional well-being and enables him to trust more and feel a greater sense of self-worth, he will develop alternate ways to gratify his need for love. These will not necessitate dependence on one other person and the possibility of disappointments; he will rely on himself and his environment for comfort and security.

The Need for Love Fuels Passion

Experiencing the need for another person's love is of fundamental importance to falling in love. To fall in love, one must also be able to idealize the attributes of the other, such as his body and features, his power, his status, or his character. These idealizations may be unrealistic and transient, but they are essential to the attraction, the desire, the longing, and the passion we feel. The intensity of this passion enables us from time to time to experience the sense of fusion and union with another person that makes falling in love such a powerful, transcendent, and sometimes frightening experience. It is difficult to imagine, however, that we would idealize another, feel passion for him, or feel merged with him if we do not need him.

Patients who have worked with me because they cannot fall in love do not usually describe profound neglect or prolonged periods of separation from their mothers in earliest childhood. What I am most often told is that their mothers were unable to convey empathy for, understanding of, or even interest in their feelings and needs, usually from the time they were six or seven years old.

If an adult recalls that his mother showed little empathy or interest in his internal life when he was six or seven, then she most likely also had difficulty responding to him in infancy and earlier childhood as well. Yet this is not necessarily the case. Deprivation in infancy and earliest childhood may be most often responsible for our inability to fall in love, but emotional neglect or deprivation that occurs in mid-childhood may also account for this difficulty.

It is possible for a mother to have been reasonably available and responsive to her child in earliest childhood, when his needs were relatively primitive and simple, but to find it difficult to tolerate the more complex emotional demands of a five- or a six-year-old. The way a child then uses what's available in his environment to soothe himself and to compensate for his mother's lack of tolerance or understanding will determine how and where he finds comfort as an adult. When the father has been rejecting or disinterested, no other caring person is available, and his mother is preoccupied or interested in her boy only when he is being a good, well-behaved, undemanding child, then he is likely to develop a high degree of self-reliance and an interest in pleasing many people, rather than in relying on any one person for his sense of security, comfort, and love. I see this scenario often in gay men who cannot fall in love.

A mother's empathic attentiveness seems to be especially important to the homosexual boy, who needs her mindfulness to compensate for what has usually been his father's disinterest, lack of appreciation, or outright rejection. The bond that he has formed with her because of their shared traits makes him especially vulnerable to her disinterest in his feelings and internal life. Unless there is an available surrogate, his mother's consistent lack of concern and lack of understanding causes him to mistrust love until he no longer finds comfort in the love of another person. As he loses touch with his need for love, he also gradually grows less able to idealize another person's attributes, thereby finding that individual less estimable and less desirable.

Charles

I previously mentioned Charles, who could not experience need for the love of another person. By the time he saw me, he had difficulty understanding even the concept of needing love. He was successful and highly intelligent but had never been able to fall in love and had been unable to sustain interest in any man for more than a few months. He mainly relied on grand physical surroundings, his achievements at work, and a large number of friends and acquaintances whom he found interesting and entertaining to soothe him and provide him with security and comfort.

His parents had just graduated from college when they married, and during Charles's childhood, they were too preoccupied with getting their emotional needs met by their own parents to adequately provide emotional sustenance for their child. As an adult, Charles felt that neither of his parents had shown much interest in his internal life. He had been close to his mother, but she was self-involved and had little tolerance for him when he needed her attention. His father had a frightening temper and emotionally withdrew if Charles dared to defy or even disagree with him. Both his mother and his father had made it clear that they wanted him to be a good, well-behaved child, a high achiever, and undemanding. By the time he was nine or ten, he believed that they were not interested in his feelings and was convinced that they could not deal with his needs. Whenever he returned home from school, he responded to his mother's inquiries about his day with "Fine," then retired to his room and fantasized that he was a prince surrounded by servants who were attentive and responsive to his every whim and wish.

Charles realized that he was attracted to other boys when he was twelve or thirteen, but he was also aware that these inclinations distracted him from pursuing his academic work, and, certain that they were incompatible with his being the good, well-behaved child his parents demanded, he put them out of his mind. He sought the approval of his peers but never felt truly close to them or as much a part of the "in crowd" as he had hoped to be. His unwanted sexual desires and the rejection by his peers further diminished his sense of self-worth.

He came out to his parents in his twenties and discovered that they were more understanding and accepting than he had expected. He dated and had sex but could not fall in love. He would date for a few months because he initially found someone attractive, but he experienced little excitement or passion. Far from idealizing his lovers, before long he lost what little interest he had in them and began to notice every defect and flaw in their appearance, character, or intellect. The men he dated, who grew aware of Charles's rapidly diminishing enthusiasm, became less emotionally available over time and sometimes lost interest in pursuing a relationship with him.

As an adult, he remained close to both his parents, relying on them for advice and counsel, speaking to them often, and seeing and traveling with them regularly. He remained particularly attached to his mother, largely unaware of his longing for the love and the attentiveness from her that she had always had difficulty expressing and that he had never experienced.

Charles wanted a relationship more because he believed he should have one than because he believed he needed one. He had met William a few months before starting therapy. Though Charles "liked him a lot," he didn't fall in love but characteristically focused on defects in William's appearance and other flaws that kept him from experiencing the desire or the passion and thereby the need that frightened him. They eventually moved in together and developed a companionable affiliation but for a long time had sex only occasionally. Charles often complained that William was, like his mother, too self-involved to meet the needs that he was gradually becoming more familiar with and better able to express. He was initially fearful of abandoning his primary reliance on work and surroundings to depend more on William, but he was determined to do so. Over the years, they developed a reasonably passionate relationship that provided them both with security and happiness.

Thomas

Thomas came to see me when he was in his fifties because he wanted to be more comfortable as a gay man. He had dated women through his young adulthood and had many one-night stands with men but had only recently acknowledged to himself that he was gay and that he wanted a close relationship with another man. He was handsome, articulate, successful, and wealthy but painfully isolated and alone. He had never fallen in love.

Thomas's father was a hard-working, successful executive, demanding and critical of his son; he had a temper that was often directed at my patient, the more sensitive and artistically gifted of two boys. Thomas's younger brother was favored by his father, so Thomas bonded closely and firmly to his mother. She was enchanted with his beauty and took care to see that he was well groomed and perfectly dressed, but she was even less able than his father was to respond to his emotional needs. In his early adolescence, adapting to their lack of concern for his internal life and to his mother's preoccupation with his appearance, Thomas devoted increasing amounts of time to the way he presented himself, to being the beautiful boy whom his mother appreciated, and to attracting others. He already mistrusted that any person could give him the love he craved.

During adolescence, Thomas became aware of his sexual desire for other boys, but he was careful not to display any interest in them because of the conviction that both his parents and his peers would find his homosexuality unacceptable. He felt isolated and alone, though he was sought after by boys and girls alike because of his good looks.

To please his parents, he dated a series of beautiful women during his young adulthood, though he felt little passion for any of them. By his late twenties, he was also having random sex with men who excited him when they admired his appearance, but he never made an effort to approach, interest, or seduce them because he found it humiliating to do so. He was convinced that they would reject him with the same lack of interest that his parents had always shown.

When I first started to work with Thomas, he was handsome and meticulously groomed but distressed because he was less able to attract men than he had been a few years earlier. His career was not flourishing as it had twenty years ago, and he could not expend the effort necessary to make himself more successful. He did, however, continue to make himself and his physical surroundings beautiful. For Thomas, as it was for Charles, the environment he created in his home was his greatest source of comfort and security.

Because he mistrusted love from another person, his main source of sexual gratification was masturbation. He fantasized about being anally penetrated, a fantasy that suggested how much he saw himself as being like his mother, along with revealing his continued attachment to her and his desire for his father's attention.

Thomas spoke to his mother daily. He was preoccupied with her health and well-being and made frequent trips to visit her to reassure himself that she was all right. He had only once discussed his sexual orientation with his parents, but neither they nor he ever brought it up again. He acknowledged that his secretiveness protected him from the judgment he feared from his father and enabled his mother to believe that he was exclusively devoted to her, which emboldened his unconscious hope that she would finally give him the love that she had been unable to provide in childhood.

Throughout his therapy, Thomas made little effort to meet men. It always seemed that his wish for a relationship was more the expression of his need for an enhancing accessory that would make him appear more attractive to others than it was the need for another's love. Even after her death, his mother remained his most important attachment.

Joseph

My patient Joseph had never been able to fall in love either. Like Thomas and Charles, he could not experience need for another's love, having long ago given up believing that he would ever find it while he was so devotedly attached to his mother. In childhood, he had learned to be self-reliant and to get soothed and comforted by the beauty of nature. He enjoyed his apartment, not for its décor, but for his view of Central Park. Like many other gay men, however, he could not find security or comfort in an intimate relationship.

His father had been a sports enthusiast who favored Joseph's more masculine older brother. Joseph had recognized in childhood that his father's antipathy was prompted by his being different from his brother: he enjoyed art, music, and nature and was uninterested in competitive contact sports. He knew his father was critical of his fearfulness and shyness, because his father refused to protect him from the taunting classmates whom Joseph frequently complained about. On one occasion, when Joseph was in the seventh grade, his father had witnessed his being teased by three or four classmates on their front lawn. When he sought the safety of the house, his father pushed him outside to fight and then watched the boys taunt and punch him.

Because of many interests and traits he shared with his mother and because of his father's rejection, Joseph was close to her. She appreciated his sensitivity and was not interested in his being an athlete. She was, however, invested in his intellectual achievements and became harshly critical if he wasn't the best and most accomplished student in his class. His achievements, he later believed, had given her a sense of fulfillment that she herself had never experienced, though Joseph never seemed able to satisfy her. Her attention made him feel wonderful and brilliant for the short time it lasted, but, ultimately, however significant his accomplishments were, they became insufficient and disappointing to her, prompting her to be dismissive and making him feel worthless and unlovable.

I started to work with Joseph when he was forty-two. He believed that neither parent had truly valued him: his father had not particularly liked him and his mother appreciated him only for his ability to be the brilliant boy she needed and expected him to be. Consequently, he had never learned to trust that he could be loved by another person. He now felt that he could not fall in love.

Joseph knew that he was attracted to other boys when he was nine or ten. He first had sex during his last year of high school, and it was then that he fell in love for the only time. In college and graduate school, because of his youthful appearance, he was able to have sex with whomever he wanted, and he described himself as having been promiscuous. After graduate school, however, unable to obtain sexual partners as easily as before, he stopped having sex and felt depressed and humiliated by his difficulty attracting partners. This initiated a period of abstinence that, except for masturbation, lasted for about ten years.

Just as Thomas and Charles had both surrounded themselves with possessions and beautiful objects that made it possible for them to continue to function without another person's love, Joseph developed self-reliance and an intricate system of self-administered rewards that enabled him to avoid having to rely on others. He ate desserts such as ice cream at planned intervals and smoked a defined number of cigarettes daily to reward himself for efforts that, he feared, would be overlooked by others. He exercised regularly—at times, excessively—to give himself a sense of control over his body. He also spent a lot of time outdoors enjoying nature, which he continued to find comforting and soothing.

In middle age he began to drink, initiated first as a part of his elaborate reward system and then to enable him to regulate his mood without depending on other people. However, after several years he recognized that he had become an alcoholic and was often out of control, especially when driving, which prompted him to join Alcoholics Anonymous and start therapy. He has been sober since that time but has spent more time each year since then close to and caring for his mother.

Each of these men had friends whom they valued, but neither had prized the love of any person except his mother. Each had adapted to the deprivation of love from both his mother and his father by learning to rely on nonhuman sources of comfort that were readily available and that he could control. Charles continued to rely on the security and the soothing comfort he obtained from his home and his financial success, Thomas relied on his outward appearance and the beauty of his apartment, and Joseph on a system of rewards, for a while on alcohol and then on natural beauty.

These men felt painfully isolated and alone because they were unable to experience need for another's love and to derive comfort from other human beings. Each remained paradoxically attached to his mother, whose earlier inability to be attentive to his feelings and to compensate for his father's rejection had caused him to have little regard for the security and the happiness that another's love could provide. Each had grown dependent on nonhuman substitutes for one person's love that eventually made falling in love impossible.

In instances when a father has been accepting, affirming, supportive, and loving of his homosexual son in childhood, the boy's early erotic attachment to him usually enables him, as an adult, to fall in love in spite of his mother's having been neglectful or uninterested in his feelings and internal life. His father's love and acceptance mitigate, though they do not entirely protect him from, the mistrust of love caused by his mother's emotional neglect. Though he may still long for his mother's love and usually continues to be deeply attached to her in the hope of getting her love, if he felt that his father loved him, he will still be able to fall in love. He usually falls in love with men who remind him of his father but then falls out of love quickly, due to the mistrust that resulted from his mother's lack of interest in his internal life and her lack of respect for his feelings and needs.

Jerome

Jerome's mother was unhappily married and depressed during his early childhood. He was the youngest of three boys, and, because of her unhappiness, she had little energy to attend to his internal life. She relied on him to make her happy, demanded that he be "good," and showed little interest in or tolerance for his feelings.

His father, unlike the fathers of most homosexual boys, had appreciated Jerome's sensitivity and gentle nature, was much more empathic and psychologically minded than his mother, and even understood from an early age that his boy was probably homosexual. He was not threatened by Jerome's atypical traits or later same-sex attractions and made an effort to spend time with Jerome in pursuits they could enjoy together. After his divorce and second marriage when Jerome was seven, he devoted as much time as possible to his children; he particularly loved and valued Jerome because of his artistic nature. Both parents were accepting when Jerome came out to them in college.

Though his father had been the more loving parent, as an adult Jerome was more attached to his mother, who had never remarried, than to his father, who by then had a second family. He felt he had more in common with her and sought her counsel about his vocational choices and the men he dated. Nevertheless, he realized that she had caused him to believe that he was of little value except as he conformed to her need for him to be a well-behaved, grown-up, dutiful, and brilliant child who made her life easier by giving her the happiness her husband had never been able to provide.

Jerome had many brief sexual liaisons and an occasional

boyfriend. He was able to fall passionately in love with men who reminded him of his father in their appearance and temperament. This passion would be short-lived, though; he soon recognized that the men he had fallen in love with were as emotionally unavailable, inattentive, selfish, and preoccupied as his mother had been. Falling out of love inevitably left him feeling bereft and disappointed, longing for someone who would remain interested in him for who he was, not just as a "cute trick."

In the next chapter, I'll explain why gay men who can fall in love but cannot stay in love, like Jerome, usually have a greater capacity to idealize other men and, at least early in their relationships, have more passion than those who cannot fall in love. They usually have not experienced from their mother the same lack of interest in their feelings as have gay men who cannot fall in love, but they, too, mistrust that love will ultimately provide them with happiness. While less fearful of loving, they are convinced that they do not deserve to be loved.

5

Staying in Love

To love somebody is not just a strong feeling—
it is a decision, it is a judgment,
it is a promise.
—*Erich Fromm*

S taying in love is not something that happens to us—we choose to make it happen. In order to stay in love, one must first decide to commit to one's partner and to the relationship itself. Although choosing to commit to another does not guarantee that a relationship will work or that one's chosen partner is the person one should be with, not being able or willing to make a commitment to him does guarantee that one will not be able to stay in love and that the relationship will not endure.

Enduring love does not occur without effort. Sometimes the effort we need to make is mundane compromise; sometimes it is a sacrifice of our own needs for our partner's; often, it is the verbal and the physical expression of our love and regard. These endeavors are motivated by our conviction that another person's love is indispensable to our ultimate happiness and, therefore, our relationship is the priority of our life.

Loving one's partner makes him feel valued, which

enables and motivates his love in turn. It is the cycle of bestowing and accepting love that nourishes and sustains any intimate relationship over time. For love to endure, we must be able to both love and be loved and to value both.

Most adults with healthy self-esteem express their self-love in committed relationships with the expectation that they will be loved and that they deserve to be loved. Those who lack self-love usually believe that commitment to another is not worth the effort it entails. They are convinced that they do not deserve to be loved because they did not feel loved in childhood.

Although making the commitment to love one other person is difficult for anyone, gay men generally have a harder time than heterosexual men do because their self-esteem is so frequently impaired and the requisite self-love is therefore lacking. I'm not referring to a compensatory, self-aggrandizing self-love that makes a person feel entitled or special, but to a self-love that's rooted in the love and the affirmation of parents that makes him feel cherished, valued, and lovable.

Gay men who cannot stay in love are not as reliant on their environment for their comfort and security as those who cannot fall in love, because they have usually had a more reliable love in childhood. Although they also mistrust the love of one person, they are better acquainted with love and are therefore less threatened by their need for love than are gay men who cannot fall in love. Instead of being totally self-reliant or looking to their home and physical surroundings for comfort, they have learned to rely on what they believe to be the more dependable pastiche of less intimate relationships: loving friends and acquaintances, extended family, their work relationships, and a variety of other men with whom they have sex. They often find it easy to fall in love and to love, at least for a while, but find it very difficult to accept another's love for long. Being loved stirs up a need for love that they do not want and believe they do not deserve.

Falling in and out of Love

A father's rejection of his homosexual son or the father's emotional withdrawal when the boy is five, six, or seven years old causes the boy to feel unlovable and, as an adult, to mistrust or devalue the love of another man. His father's rejection and favoring of his siblings often prompts a gay adult to be competitive with his partner, as he was with the siblings his father preferred, further contributing to the difficulty he has staying committed and attached to any lover. The rejection that most homosexual boys experience later in adolescence from peers, their unrequited crushes on straight boys, and the social bias that teaches them that longing for another man is bad, sinful, or perverse, all reinforce and may intensify their earlier mistrust of love and their belief that they will not get the love they need.

Many gay men who cannot stay in love protect themselves from committing to another by falling in and then out of love. When they are alone, they feel unlovable or defective, so they date frantically and have sex with a variety of men, attempting to garner reassurance of their attractiveness and lovability by getting others to fall in love with them. They fall in love, and do so often, but the reassurance that comes from these relationships is short-lived. Sooner rather than later, they become concerned that they need too much, that they will not get the love they want, or that their lovers will be turned off by their neediness. Frightened that they will again be rejected and hurt as they were by their fathers, they fall out of love.

Steven

Steven was an intellectually gifted man in his late thirties whose talent and intelligence had been appreciated by his well-educated mother, while his father, who seemed to have disdain for him, had been more loving and attentive to both his older sister and his athletic younger brother. Steven came to see me because of his inability to stay in love with any of his four previous lovers. The duration of his longest relationship had been two years.

His father was a successful executive whose aggressive style was acknowledged and respected throughout the business community. Steven was shy and unathletic and preferred playing with neighborhood girls or his older sister to the other boys. He was too shy in grade school or high school to be one of the more popular boys, though he usually had his own clique composed of bright girls who found him cute, and some boys who found him funny or smart.

Steven's father didn't think he was cute or funny and complained that he was a sissy. Whenever his father came home from work, Steven eagerly tried to crawl into his father's lap to snuggle, even when he was nine or ten. His father, irritated, pushed him away. His mother was warmer and much kinder. She admired his gentle, soft qualities and intellectual prowess, but her attention and affection did not help. She was unable or unwilling to protect him from his father. Over time, hurt and angered by his father's continued dismissiveness and obvious favoring of his other siblings, Steven angrily turned away from his father. In adolescence, aware that his masturbation fantasies were usually of men like his father and sometimes of his father, he attempted to fantasize about someone else, even women, whom he tried to date for a while.

When he first started therapy with me, he spent a considerable amount of time talking about his father: how hateful, cruel, and dismissive his father was. He often told me how much he hated his father, who, not surprisingly, did not speak to him for two years after Steven came out in his midtwenties.

Steven had no difficulty falling in love, but he always fell for men who reminded him of his father. They were initially aggressive and critical and usually had his father's natural masculinity and dark complexion. Inevitably, as his lovers became more attentive and kind, Steven began to call their attention to the other men whom he found to be more attractive than them and then to have sex outside of his relationship. Eventually, Steven cruelly rejected his boyfriends before they could reject him. Our work together over many years helped to clarify his longing for his father's love, acceptance, and respect and how his denial of this longing and unremitting anger was displaced onto his lovers, making it impossible for him to stay committed and attached to them.

.　　.　　.

The bond with a mother who is loving and affirming may protect a homosexual boy from the painful consequences of his father's rejection. As we saw in the previous chapter, however, she may exploit the relationship to serve her own needs. She might treat him as an extension of herself, look to him to fulfill her own frustrated longings or ambitions, or neglect his struggle for autonomy and independence, causing him to experience his intimate relationships as an unbearable constraint or an infringement on his freedom.

Sometimes a mother may be unconsciously seductive or too physical with her homosexual boy in order to counter her concern that he is homosexual or her fear that her close emotional connection may have caused his homosexuality. An adult gay man may react to his mother having been sexually provocative by finding it difficult to be sexual with anyone with whom he maintains an intimate, loving emotional connection, by seeking sex outside of his relationship or by falling out of love.

Stuart

Stuart was in his early thirties when he came for therapy, seeking help because he felt chronically anxious and depressed. He was dissatisfied with his relationship of two years and felt confined by it. He complained that he was no longer in love and was eager to rediscover the passion for his partner that he had experienced when they first met.

He was the oldest of two children. As a child, he was very attached to his mother, who always told him how much she adored him; how handsome, talented, and smart he was; and what a good child he was. She was physically affectionate, making him uncomfortable with her constant touching, hugs, and kisses. Stuart saw his father as strong and masculine but emotionally distant, preoccupied with work, and rejecting. His parents' marriage, he believed, had never been happy. His sensitivity, emotionality, and lack of interest in sports made him different from his father, who was an amateur athlete. The bond with his mother and her physical attention had contributed, he believed, to his father's jealousy, distance, and preference for a younger sibling.

Their closeness, her troubled marriage, and his parents' frequent and frightening vociferous arguments had all fostered Stuart's belief that his mother needed him to make her life happier and better. Because he had tried to be good, to accommodate to her needs, and to do everything he could to make her life easier, he was furious whenever she paid attention to his sister or his father. To be a good boy, however, he had to repress or inhibit his jealousy, which then resurfaced destructively in his adult relationships.

By the age of eight or nine, he had recognized his attraction to his muscular father and to other older men, as well as to boys his own age, but to please both his parents he dated girls in high school. In his junior year, however, he began to have anonymous sex at a mall near his school, which provided him with a sense of his attractiveness and his independence from his mother by defying her need for him to continue to be close and to be good. That the sex was anonymous enabled him to experience physical closeness to boys and men without evoking a restricting sense of emotional attachment or a perception that he was betraying his mother.

When Stuart started therapy, he complained of feeling confined by his relationship with the man he had fallen in love with three years previously. He was also jealous of his partner's attention to colleagues and friends, which sometimes reminded him of his mother's attention to his younger sister and at times of his father's. He had increasingly frequent anonymous sexual encounters outside of his relationship to mitigate his jealousy and to assert his freedom from the constraints he experienced. The relationship was deteriorating because each partner felt increasingly alienated and angry.

After breaking up, Stuart found himself once again eager to be in a relationship, unaware of his wish to re-evoke the close earlier attachment to his mother. He soon fell in love with a young man who was devoted, emotionally generous, and thoughtful, but once again Stuart felt limited and confined by the relationship. He became irritated and increasingly distant, occasioned at times by his partner's devotion and at other times by jealousy of his partner's attention to friends and colleagues. He again began to have sex outside of the relationship in order to assert his freedom and to feel less confined and less restricted by his partner. It also enabled him to be less burdened by his jealousy. Of course, the excitement and the adventure of sex with strangers had the effect of making him even less interested in his lover.

He experienced the loss of freedom in his relationship with his partners to be distressing, just as he had with his mother. And just as he had needed to free himself from his mother as an adolescent, he wanted freedom from the confining gaze of his adoring partners. He found relief in his affairs and in random sex, which devalued his lovers and, in doing so, maintained the primacy of his mother in his emotional life.

Larry

Those who believe that loving another and being loved are valuable and essential to their happiness find that the freedom they surrender in committing to a partner and a relationship—that is, the necessary compromises, sacrifices, and striving for fidelity—is worthwhile. "The freedoms that they lose in accommodating to one another," Irving Singer wrote, "will seem peripheral to what they care about most." Some gay men who cannot commit to another person because they find a relationship too limiting or too burdensome feel confined, not only by memories of their mothers' anomalous love, but by their own need for the parental love that they disavowed long ago and that now makes them angry.

Larry came for therapy when he was in his late twenties because of the breakup of his marriage of eight years. He and his wife had been emotionally close, but there had been little sex, and he now wanted to experience his sexual passion by living as an openly gay man.

Larry's father had been emotionally distant and often physically absent, protecting himself from his depressed and irritable wife by immersing himself in his work. He clearly favored Larry's older sibling, a more robust, athletic, typical boy. Larry was quiet, studious, and intellectual, preferring the company of girls to the more aggressive neighborhood boys. He was close to his depressed and sometimes overly demonstrative, clinging mother, who was more accepting and who needed him to compensate for her unhappy life. From quite early on, he had felt confined by her demands on him to be a good and obedient boy. She did not permit him to express his frustration, anger, or needs, and she had little interest in his feelings or in knowing who he really was.

In his adolescence, Larry dated and had sex with girls to please his parents, although he fantasized about boys and was aware of his attraction to boys in his class. Yet the idea of being homosexual was anathema to him. It did not conform to his religious upbringing or to fulfilling his parents' expectations.

He lived at home during college because of financial constraints and because his mother wanted him nearby. Marriage was, he believed, the only way he could escape his mother's demands for his continued closeness. It did serve this purpose, but he felt a frightening loss of freedom after his marriage, partly due to his seeing the relationship as demanding and confining like the one with his mother, and partly because he then wanted to begin to have sex with men.

Larry had no trouble meeting other men for sex because of his natural good looks, charm, and affable ways. After separating from his wife, however, and despite wanting a relationship, he found himself more and more inhibited. He relied on alcohol, cocaine, and crystal methamphetamine to feel less inhibited and more attractive to the men he met. Shortly after starting therapy, he met John, an attractive man who also wanted a committed, monogamous relationship. After they lived together a few months, Larry again felt confined by the obligations of this relationship and limited by the need to care about his partner, as he had felt for so many years by his mother.

He competed with his lover for other people's attention, which was reminiscent of his competition with and jealousy of his older brother. He felt an unbearable loss of freedom, again seeking nights away from John, relying on alcohol and cocaine in order to meet other men and occasionally on crystal meth to overcome his anxiety and to temporarily increase his sense of self-worth. His relationship, of course, rapidly deteriorated, and John left him.

Larry had the capacity, the courage, and an appealing eagerness to confront and do something about his problems. He gradually felt good enough about himself to stop relying so heavily on alcohol and drugs. Eventually, he met another man with whom he fell in love. They have been living together happily, although Larry is continuing to struggle with his anxiety about the responsibilities of commitment and about the loss of freedom that his committed relationship entails.

Searching for the Perfect Partner

Some of the men who fall in and out of love protect themselves from being hurt or from not getting what they need by searching for the "perfect" partner. They are always looking for someone who is better than the man they are currently with—someone who is great looking and terrifically smart with a better job and the social status to provide them with the value that they believe they lack. Sometimes they find a new partner with just the assets they are looking for, but that person's capacity for love, compassion, or commitment is not high on their list of valued attributes. A gay man who is searching for the perfect partner does not value or trust love at all. He has usually been hurt by his father's rejection and by his mother's inattentiveness to his feelings or disrespect for his need for autonomy. He does not search for someone who is loving or caring because he is convinced that he is not worth the love such a person could provide. The superficial attributes that he values and seeks turn out to be poor substitutes for love, so once again he is disappointed. The relationship inevitably fulfills his unconscious conviction that he is unlovable and that no person can provide the love he needs.

William

William illustrates how the fear of commitment may be manifest in a gay man's relentless search for the perfect partner and how this search keeps him from staying in love. William was constantly looking for someone whose intellect and social position were better than his own and better than those of whoever he was with at the time.

William's father had been rejecting, distant, and unavailable, and his mother was often cruel, ridiculing William for needing her too much. She admired his intelligence, which bonded them early, but both parents preferred his four-years-younger sister.

Contributing to their preference for the younger sibling was William's typical lack of enthusiasm for rough play, his pleasure in dramatic performance—his own and others'—and his preference for playing with girls. Emotional abandonment by both parents after the birth of his sister, and especially his father's withdrawal and indifference, made William believe early in childhood that he must be unworthy of love because he had been bad.

Academic achievement was his sole means of garnering the attention and the love that he unconsciously longed for and needed. He was increasingly aware of the nature of his sexuality in adolescence and fearful of rejection by his peers, and his achievements helped him to feel less vulnerable to their criticism and ridicule.

As an adult, his considerable accomplishments compensated for his feeling unloved and unappreciated, but whenever he was alone, he again felt defective; for reassurance he would search the Internet for sex or a date. Although he always found boyfriends, he fell out of love with each one quickly. Convinced that he would be hurt, he could not commit to anyone. He quickly found fault with every man he fell in love with: they were not successful enough, not socially prominent enough, not intellectual enough, or too encumbered by financial worries. He was frightened by his reliance on one person's love and diffused his need through sex with others whom he found more attractive than his partner. Each of his lovers eventually grew to believe, as William had been made to feel as a child, that he was unimportant, inadequate, and not valued.

Jacob

At the start of his therapy, Jacob was wary of commitment because he mistrusted and devalued love. His fear of commitment was manifested not by falling in and out of love like

William but by staying in love until each of his partners rejected him.

Jacob told me that he was eager to find a partner and that he was looking for someone "perfect," someone who could make him feel worthwhile. To convince himself that the man he was with was perfect, he would idealize this individual's appearance and intelligence but inevitably would find the man to be unavailable and unable to return his love. In a matter of months, he recognized that the man whose "perfection" had enabled him to fall in love was unwilling or unable to love him, making the relationship uneven and unworkable. The intensity of love that he had experienced early on was never matched or reciprocated. The idealizations that had made him fall in love had also made it impossible for him to recognize the emotional inadequacies of his partner, which eventually caused him again to feel unloved.

Jacob had a typical homosexual boy's childhood, preferring to play with girls and shying away from aggressive play. His father clearly preferred Jacob's more athletic younger brother and divorced his wife because of long-standing marital difficulties when Jacob was an adolescent. Nevertheless, Jacob believed that his father had left because his father disliked him.

Jacob was close to his mother, who appreciated his sensitivity and artistic talents. She needed him to remain bonded to her, though, to compensate for her unhappy relationship with his father and later for her unhappiness with her new husband. When she attempted to demonstrate her love, she was often too affectionate: hugging, kissing, and stroking his head and neck. She worried later that their intimacy had contributed to his feminine traits, and, as his father had done, she also admonished him to be more like other boys. The bond he experienced with her was confusing: he was close to her because they shared common traits and interests, but she wanted him to be more the man of the family, more of a companion, and more her savior than he was ever capable of being.

Jacob had been hurt by his father's rejection and later by his mother's lack of respect for his increasing need to be independent. In his adult love relationships, he was intent on recovering the feeling of closeness he had with his mother, especially before her unhappy second marriage, by initially falling blissfully in love. However, as his idealizations inevitably began to falter, he found himself confined by these relationships and crushingly disappointed by his lovers' inability to care about him. He had rediscovered the painful experience of once again loving someone who rejected him as his father had, and he felt confined and frightened by his lovers just as he had felt with his mother. The idealizations that initially made falling in love so wonderful had made staying in love impossible.

It is commonly believed that the difficulty in committing to another and staying in love with him are caused by one's inability to give love to him. I am convinced, however, that most gay men find it harder to accept love than to give it, because being loved evokes their repudiated and conflicted need for love more readily than loving does.

Michael

Michael came to see me when he was in his midthirties because he could not stay in love. He was handsome, charming, articulate, outgoing, and intelligent, a man others readily desired and easily fell in love with. Although he could be financially and emotionally generous, his need for another's love made him intensely anxious, and he recognized that he could not permit another man to love him for long. This made committing to a lover, and therefore staying in love, impossible.

Michael's father had been distant, authoritarian, rejecting, and emotionally withdrawn, as his own father had been before him. Michael had adored his mother; however, she had been preoccupied with her friends and busy social life to the neglect of the emotional needs of Michael and his older brother. She had neither the temperament nor the desire to take care of her children. Michael had the looks and the intelligence that made him desirable in this family, so he was the sole recipient of his mother's fleeting, momentary attention. Yet she was, he believed, interested in him only for these superficial attributes that were so pleasing to her and that enhanced her feelings about herself. Her limited and selfish attention was insufficient. Michael had felt unloved.

When he was five or six, he began to evidence traits that his father disdained: a lack of interest in rough play and sports, and an enthusiasm for music and theater. He was emotionally expressive and carried his books, his father told him, held to his chest like a girl. His mother had neither the interest nor the inclination to provide support; he consequently believed she, too, was disappointed in him. In late childhood and early adolescence, like most homosexual boys, Michael was rebuffed by his peers and remained an outsider until his rebellious behavior in the last two years of high school made him more acceptable to boys of his own age, if not to his teachers. To curry the favor of his class-mates, and because of the shame of his burgeoning same-sex impulses, he dated girls in high school and his early years in college.

By the time he came to see me, Michael's accustomed rebelliousness in the service of his fear of rejection and poor self-regard had made his chosen vocation and his relation-ships problematic. He often acted arrogantly in an attempt to conceal from himself and others a conviction that he was unlovable. He disappointed those who demonstrated any interest in him and, when rebuffed or rejected, felt worthless and hopeless.

Michael preferred one-night stands and casual relation-ships; their frequency and novelty reassured him of his con-tinuing attractiveness and kept him from being angered by anyone's sustained interest. He would fall in love, but once a relationship evolved from being only sexual and his partner demonstrated any emotional attachment, Michael withdrew and wanted to "take a break." The more a lover expressed affection, the more he evoked Michael's unwelcome need for love, his rage at the person eliciting it, and an irresistible desire to have sex with other men. His lovers eventually expe-rienced themselves as unwanted and unnecessary for his hap-piness, just as Michael had felt with his mother and his father.

Unfortunately, his experience with me in therapy did not help him to overcome his mistrust of love. He viewed me as being like his parents, not truly interested in him. My efforts to help were, he believed, for my benefit alone—to prove I was a good therapist. He attempted to disappoint me and obstruct my efforts to help, and, ultimately, after several years he left treatment, once again discouraged.

Michael did not believe that happiness could possibly evolve from an ongoing relationship. Though he had initially been committed to therapy because he wanted to be able to have a relationship, he did not feel lovable or deserving enough to sustain his commitment to it and was convinced that he would eventually be emotionally hurt by my rejection. Because he could not believe that he needed another's love, he sabotaged my efforts to care for or about him, just as he had everyone else's.

Gay men who have a problem staying in love do not trust that the love of one person is a safe or reliable way to achieve happiness. They do not possess the love of self that is necessary to accept another's love except for relatively short periods of time.

Although our brains have stored the memories connected with feelings from our childhood experiences of love, these imprinted experiences need not dominate the way we as adults continue to love and process the love of others. It is possible to redo old memories of a father's rejection or a mother's selfish and confining love by having new and different experiences of love. Therapy can begin to revise these memories, and it can begin to alter an impoverished self-love.

6

How Therapy
Works

We must become aware in order to choose the
good—but no awareness will help us if we have
lost the capacity to be moved by the distress of
another human being, by the friendly gaze of
another person, by the greenness of grass.
—*Erich Fromm*

P sychotherapy is a good and effective way to learn that love is possible. The most helpful type of psychotherapy will be one in which a patient can explore the reasons for and origins of his difficulties but can also perceive and experience the loving attitude of his therapist.

Three features of therapy make it work. The best known is that a person attempts to talk honestly to his therapist without censoring his thoughts, enabling unconscious or barely conscious memories and feelings to become more available to him with the help of his therapist's clarifications and interpretations. The relationship one had as a child with his parents and the ways he experienced their love will result in his responding in adult intimate relationships as he had learned to do as a child. Of course, by the time he seeks therapy, additional experiences with peers and friends have also shaped his behavior and attitudes about love, but, unless a person gains some understanding of his earlier relationships with his parents, the adaptations he made to secure his mother's and his father's love continue to be the main influences on the way he loves and accepts love. As he becomes more aware of repressed thoughts and feelings about a parental love that was inconsistent or unreliable or where his needs did not matter, a person will likely become more discerning of those whose love is unreliable, will over time find more men who are capable of loving, and will eventually recognize that love can potentially be more nourishing than he had previously believed. The intellectual understanding of how one's past has influenced one's current feelings about love, however, is only a first step.

The Importance of Transference

Because of the nature and the structure of the therapeutic situation, a patient will eventually perceive his therapist as reacting like either or both of his parents. Transferring these old feelings to the therapist is an essential element of any good therapy. If a therapist is caring and concerned about his patient's happiness and attempts to focus on the patient to the relative exclusion of himself and his own needs, transferences are bound to occur. Since the therapeutic attitude of caring and concern is inherently more similar in our culture to the parental role of a mother than of a father, after a period of time, whether the therapist is a man or a woman, gay or straight, he is likely to evoke recollections of the patient's mother. However, the authority consigned to a physician or therapist in our society, as well as the patient coming to his therapist's office for appointments at an established time and paying for his treatment, usually, sooner or later, invite recollections of his father. Over time, these maternal and paternal transferences will be projected onto the therapist if his or her empathy, concern for the patient, nonjudgmental attitude, and curiosity create a safe environment that inevitably encourages them. These transferences, when they are clarified, provide immediate, important, and convincing illustrations of not only how the patient perceived his parents and how he reacted to them, but of how they influence his other relationships, particularly the most intimate ones.

A man in his early forties came to see me because he had not been able to sustain a relationship for more than a few months. He described his childhood as having been happy and his relationship with both parents as good, but his reaction to me from early in his therapy belied these statements. No matter how carefully, kindly, and thoughtfully I attempted to clarify his thoughts or feelings, he was convinced that I was putting him down and denigrating his intelligence. We learned after a time that his reaction to me was a manifestation of a paternal transference: his father had competed with him, consistently challenging his knowledge, and humiliating him by making him feel uninformed and inadequate. The transference of feelings from these experiences enabled me to illustrate to my patient how his relationship with his father contributed to his mistrust of other men, to the difficulty he had permitting anyone to love him, and, if they did love him, to his finding ways to humiliate them as he had been humiliated.

The problems that gay men have loving and accepting love are often exacerbated by social bias, but they are largely caused by the way they have been treated and raised by their parents. Most gay men who seek help, however, are initially inclined to believe that their problems with loving other men have been caused *solely* by social bias and by the antipathy or the rejection they encountered from peers during adolescence and young adulthood. While I do not minimize the pain caused by peer rejection and the cultural bias against same-sex love, they usually serve to reinforce and substantiate the low self-regard that was produced by the parents' earlier lack of tolerance and understanding. When a mother and a father accept their homosexual boy and he has been raised in an atmosphere of respect, tolerance, and love, he will feel relatively unencumbered by later rejections. Those who are inclined to believe that their peers' rejections in adolescence, along with current prejudice and social inequality, are the sole reasons for their difficulty falling in love usually do so to obscure painful memories of the anomalous nature of their parents' love, which continues to exert a profound effect on their capacity to love and be loved.

The Transferences of Gay Men

The relationships that homosexual boys have had with their parents prompt specific transferences that may not be exclusive to gay men but are very commonly seen in treating them. One is that they may experience the therapist as being rejecting, belittling, or dismissive. This type of transference usually derives from a gay man's experience with a father who was angry and competitive with him because of his close bond to his mother. This was the case with the patient I just described.

For most gay men, however, feeling humiliated or rejected by the therapist is more complicated, deriving from the rejection of a father who dismissively thought of his son as a sissy.

Michael, whom I discussed in the last chapter, was a man I liked and enjoyed working with. He was convinced, however, that I did not like him because he was not as successful as my other patients. His father had been consistently dismissive and rejecting, labeling him "girly" or "phony" and expressing displeasure at his interest in the arts, his posture, and his feminine gait. His father's preference for Michael's siblings was an important source of his low self-esteem and of the dismaying lack of respect he experienced from me and in most of his other relationships.

Another type of paternal transference often seen with gay men evolves from their early, usually unconscious, sexual feelings for fathers who were rejecting or dismissive. Consequently, some of these men, as adults, experience rejection and humiliation as the only attitude or behavior that they find sexually arousing. When they start to feel close to their therapists, they may also unconsciously experience similar erotic feelings; the more a therapist tries to be helpful, the more some feel denigrated or humiliated. Other gay men who had rejecting fathers may respond to their increasing attachment to the therapist by withdrawing or by dismissively perceiving the therapy and the therapist to be boring or uninformative. Similarly, in an intimate, romantic relationship where, because of the earlier ties to a rejecting father, it is necessary to experience rejection or humiliation in order for one's partner to remain sexually attractive, the partner who is loving and attentive may no longer be interesting, desirable, or exciting.

Some gay men, as we have seen, have developmental issues related to close attachments to their mothers. This type of bond to the mother may also influence the way a gay man perceives his therapist. He often resents having to keep regular appointments because of his mother's old demand that he be good and well-behaved. He is quick to discern how the therapist wants him to comport himself and soon believes that the therapist is imposing a prescription for behavior to which he must subscribe or, like his mother, the therapist will no longer care about him. These are usually the transferences of a mother who used her homosexual boy and his close bond with her to gratify her own needs, disregarding or discouraging the child's developmental strivings for independence.

Anger or withdrawal concerning the therapist's vacations or unanticipated absences may be due to a revival of old anxieties about separation from one's mother, or the therapist's interruptions may be used to confirm the conviction that like the patient's mother, the therapist is selfishly interested only in himself and his own well-being. Sometimes anger about separations expresses a patient's concern that he has done something wrong and that these interruptions would not have occurred had he not displeased his therapist. It is essential that a therapist permit these reactions to be verbalized and that he not be too reassuring or too quick to correct a misperception, for such interventions may make it difficult for the patient to see how he is misinterpreting a current situation, where his feelings are coming from, and how he may be responding in similar ways in other intimate relationships. In spite of their therapist's best efforts, some patients leave treatment abruptly and prematurely to assert their independence, out of anxiety about their growing dependence or in anger over what they experience to be the therapist's unreasonable demands.

I believe it is usually beneficial for gay men to work with gay therapists. I continue to be convinced of this, even though there are now more gay role models available to gay men, and straight therapists are no longer as inclined to view their patients' homosexuality as deviant or mutable as they were twenty or even ten years ago. A gay therapist who is knowledgeable about human development; who is also inquisitive, respectful, caring, and focused; and who is familiar with his patients' experiences and has successfully struggled with his own problems in his own intimate relationships is more likely than a straight therapist to be able to empathize with his gay patients and to help them with their difficulties with falling in love or staying in love. Although some classical Freudian analysts have maintained that a transference cannot develop if a gay patient knows his therapist is also gay, the transference will be unaffected by knowledge of his therapist's sexual orientation as long as both the therapist and his patient believe it is important to permit these feelings to develop and to understand them.

A Therapist's Loving Attitude

The recollection and the comprehension of old experiences, even when these are combined with an indispensable attention to the transference, are by themselves generally not enough to help patients with their difficulties falling in love or staying in love. If therapy is to change ungratifying patterns of loving, the therapist needs to have an attitude that his patient perceives as caring and loving. The experience of a therapist's love usually occurs over time as a patient becomes increasingly aware of his therapist's interest in his well-being and happiness, which is conveyed through empathy, understanding, respect, concern, and thoughtfulness. Hopefully, the patient will internalize this loving attitude, which will provide the foundation for a new perception of and a different view of love from the one he formed in childhood. It is often necessary to experience a therapist's loving attitude over a sustained period of time to acquire enough trust to love another person and to accept another's love.

If the therapist's love is important in changing his patient's perceptions about love and intimacy, should he not explicitly verbalize and demonstrate it? It is helpful for a therapist to be interactive and not passive and unresponsive, but verbal expressions of affection, excessive self-revelation, and giving advice frequently to reassure one's patient that he cares about him may make a patient feel as if he is not being listened to or that the therapist is acting like his mother, who could not permit him to develop his own separate identity. Expressions of affection and other reassurances that are too explicit, too frequent, or too quickly offered not only interfere with the development and the understanding of the transference, they may also undermine a patient's belief in his capacity to master his conflicts and frustrations on his own and may lead him to expect continuing reassurance, which, when not forthcoming, might make him feel rejected. Even the occasional physical demonstration of affection, like a hug, prompts some patients to expect or to hope that their therapists will meet all of their emotional or sexual needs, leading to disappointment, frustration, and anger when the therapists are unable or unwilling to do so.

While I do not believe that physical demonstrations of caring are ever useful, there are times when explicit verbal expression of concern may help, such as when the patient has experienced significant trauma or loss. If a therapist is not forthcoming at these times, the patient will surmise that he is unempathic or uncaring. Withholding in order to maintain neutrality does not convey concern. It is thoughtless and unloving.

Expressing support and concern when there has been a significant trauma or loss seems to be common sense, but many psychoanalysts and analytically oriented therapists are still reluctant to offer such reassurance. Even at times of crisis, they may feel it appropriate to be neutral "mirrors" of their patients' feelings. Their attitude is derived from Freud's admonition for analysts to model themselves during psychoanalytic treatment "on the surgeon who puts aside all his feelings, even his own sympathy . . . " to be a mirror of his patient's conflict, sharing with them "nothing but what is shown to him."

Freud made these comments because he was concerned about male analysts who were tempted to have sex with their female patients, but many classical Freudian analysts still act as if he had designated the attitude they should maintain with all patients in all situations. The therapist or the analyst who is as mirroring and detached as Freud seemed to advocate will not be therapeutic for patients who have problems with love and intimacy. A therapist who is most effective in treating these problems is caringly interactive without being unduly self-revelatory or intrusive, but he is also constantly attentive to the effect of these interactions on the way his patient thinks about himself, about the therapist, and about other people. This technique is borrowed not only from Freud but from other analysts as well.

Sandor Ferenczi, one of Freud's early followers, reacting to what he believed to be the harmful effects of the unnatural coldness of most analysts who followed Freud's "mirror" dictum, emphasized the therapeutic importance of the analyst as a real person but then, I believe, incorrectly recommended direct and active loving interventions in order to provide traumatized patients with the love they had been deprived of as children. His recommendations led some therapists to manipulate their patients to gratify their own needs, to their bringing too much of themselves to the relationship, and to the eventual disappointment of patients who expected too much from their therapists. Ferenczi did make an essential contribution to analytic technique by recognizing that the relationship with the analyst or the therapist is a real one and that this real relationship could have a profound and therapeutic effect on his patients.

Somewhat later, Franz Alexander wrote that psychoanalysis is in fact a "corrective emotional experience" and that "the essence of the therapeutic process consists of the difference between the physician's reaction and that of the parents, parent substitutes, and/or siblings."

Alexander was often misunderstood to be advocating, as Ferenczi had, that the analyst adopt a parental role, but he was instead emphasizing that the analyst's consistency, empathy, and caring provide the "favorable kind of emotional climate" that would enable patients to observe that these responses were usually quite different from the way their parents had originally treated them. This would also facilitate patients' recognizing the difference between transference and the analyst's actual behavior.

Hans Loewald, a classical Freudian, responding to the increasingly intellectualistic, authoritarian, and impersonal psychoanalysis of the 1960s, wrote that an analyst is neutral and objective only in the sense that he avoids being pulled by his patient into being either like a depriving, critical parent as patients will tempt him to do or being pulled into acting like the opposite of them, that is, overtly loving, in order to provide patients with what they had been deprived of, as Ferenczi had suggested. Loewald recognized that the analyst becomes a "new object" in the life of his patient, not by being the parent whom the patient did not have but by showing his love and respect for the developmental challenges his patient confronted. Loewald was convinced, as am I, that it is the gradual trust that evolves over time that enables a patient to see his therapist as a "new object" and to forge a new relationship with the therapist that is quite unlike the one he had with his parents. This relationship "serves as a focal point for the establishment of healthier object relations in the patient's real life."

The Compulsion to Repeat
Old Relationships

Why are human beings inclined to repeat painful as well as loving aspects of their early relationships with their mothers and their fathers, and why is it so difficult to change the harmful, destructive ways we learned to love and accept love?

The neurophysiological explanation for the tendency to repeat these old patterns is that feelings connected with our early experiences are stored in the portion of the brain known as the limbic system. An early "love" that was inattentive, indifferent, or rejecting is imprinted on the young, impressionable brain just as good and caring parental love is imprinted, providing the prototype for what emotional relatedness, intimacy, and attachment feel like. Lewis, Amini, and Lannon write that "Anomalous love—one where needs don't matter or where love is suffocating or autonomy intolerable—makes its ineradicable limbic stamp. Healthy loving then becomes incomprehensible."

The psychological explanation for our repeating unpleasant experiences as well as good ones is that we seek out old feelings about love because they are familiar—we know what to expect and how to react, even though repeating these experiences may cause our relationships to be miserable. Knowing what to expect and repeating familiar ways of responding give us the illusion of control over past unhappiness by re-creating it in the present with the hope that now we can make it right.

The comfort we obtain from being exposed to people who behave in familiar ways and the comfort we derive from familiar ways of adapting to this behavior make it difficult to change both the types of people we love and our responses to them. For these reasons, simply understanding why someone is impaired in his ability to love is not enough to help him resolve these difficulties. Understanding alone does not lead to change. The behaviors we have learned in childhood and honed in adolescence to protect ourselves from disappointment and rejection become habitual and must be replaced by new experiences that enable us to have new hopes, new convictions, and new expectations.

We cannot love another or accept his love until we feel deserving of it. Although an initial step to improving self-esteem occurs through understanding how and why we feel unloved, the sense of our increased self-worth indispensably comes from internalizing the therapist's loving attitude. Only then can we begin to trust that a new, unfamiliar type of love is possible. Because, over time, we have begun to believe through our relationship with an understanding, empathic, and caring therapist that we must deserve love and that it will be possible to experience love, we will usually find the courage to seek love from others and to develop the self-discipline necessary to overcome our old inclinations to sabotage it. Both courage and self-discipline are by-products of a therapy that has increased a person's self-love, and both are requisite for the pursuit and maintenance of new, better, and unfamiliar love.

Jack

A thirty-five-year-old man came to treatment because he was unable to sustain a loving relationship over any significant period of time. He wanted to be able to do so and was convinced that his many brief affairs contributed to his poor self-regard and hopelessness.

Jack had been raised by parents who had physical disabilities, as well as emotional problems that made them unable to provide him and his younger siblings with the love and the care they needed. He spent his childhood trying not to distress his parents, adapting to their disabilities, their self-absorption, and their neglect by learning not to expect what they could not provide. At an early age he became self-reliant.

Embarrassed by his parents' inability to take care of him and by his father's preference for his siblings, Jack unconsciously believed that he was getting the poor care he deserved and that he was bad and unlovable. He tried to hide his shame from his neighbors, teachers, and peers by making an effort to seem well put-together: he dressed neatly, prepared his homework scrupulously, and tried to look carefree and happy.

At age eleven or twelve, he started to recognize his attraction to boys in his class, and he focused on this sexual interest as the reason he had been neglected by his parents and felt so much shame. Because he had grown to believe that his sexual desire was the cause of his neglect and because his attraction to other boys evoked his unwanted need for them, he put the sexual thoughts and feelings out of his mind. He was so successful at diverting himself from these thoughts that he did not masturbate while he was in high school.

After leaving home to attend college, he felt enough physical and emotional distance from the humiliation of needing his unresponsive parents that he was able to tolerate his sexual desire. He began to masturbate and then to experiment sexually with other young men; late in college, he met a man a few years older than he was with whom he had a short relationship. Jack remained, however, mistrustful and distant, and the relationship gradually deteriorated.

Despite his good looks and high intelligence, as an adult

Jack was convinced that if he showed how much he needed another person, he would be rejected, so he was usually attracted to men who were as familiarly and tantalizingly unavailable as his father had been. And, in unconscious retaliation for his childhood neglect, either he found those who desired him undesirable or he withheld his affection, causing them to believe that he neither needed nor desired them.

During the first two years of his psychotherapy, Jack's relationship with me was correct but strikingly detached. I loved the courageous way in which he engaged the struggle to understand himself in order to be happier. I have no doubt that he could see that I cared for and about him. Nevertheless, he reacted to me as if I were a dispenser of valuable information and not a person whom he could trust and rely upon. He listened carefully but would not take much from me. He seldom asked for or about anything; he did not appear to want, expect, or need anything.

Jack conveyed in these ways, and through his controlled posture and inexpressive tone, that he was afraid to feel dependent and was angry over what he believed to be the unreliable nature of my love, especially at times of separation when he routinely missed appointments, offering the rationalizations of oversleeping or being too busy. My calling attention to these responses enabled Jack, over several years, to appreciate that his reaction to me more accurately reflected his adaptation to both his mother's and his father's neglect than to the way I was treating him. Gradually, he began to recognize that I was more concerned about his well-being and happiness than he had believed. Over time, he began to trust me enough to speak about his longing to be loved. His experience in therapy had begun to alter his childhood experience of love.

In his third year of therapy, Jack met an attractive, outgoing, charming man who unfortunately proved to be, in his own way, as self-involved and neglectful as Jack's parents had been. Once again, a relationship had evoked disappointment, loss, and a sense of hopelessness. Articulating his anger and disappointment enabled Jack to understand how this man had brought up familiar feelings of rejection in him. Jack was also angry at me for not having been more helpful, and, because he was expressing his anger, he feared that I would not continue to be caring and understanding and I would lose interest in helping him.

A year after breaking up with the man, he met Matt, who did have the capacity to care about him. They fell in love and after two years moved in together. Matt's love eventually enabled Jack to revise his old feelings about love.

It is this love of another person over a long period of time that finally and unequivocally establishes a new and different understanding of what love is and what it feels like. It is this love of one person over time that is the only lasting therapy for problems of love. A successful psychotherapy can make this love possible.

7

The Therapeutic
Power of Love

Trust is a big word. It is the seed whence grow
faith, hope and love, and the fruit which ripens
out of them. It is the very simplest and just for
that the most difficult.
—*Franz Rosenzweig*

The love of parents in childhood forms the template on which we pattern all our intimate adult relationships, making it difficult, though not impossible, to change what we have learned about love. A gay man who, as a child, felt that his father's love was dismissive and his mother's selfish and unempathic, and as an adolescent experienced the rejection of unrequited love and later society's bias against homosexual love and relationships, is often unable to either fall in love or to sustain love. Until he understands his importunate mistrust of love and relationships, he may deny that he needs love at all. Until he understands his attraction to old and familiar experiences of love, he will be inclined to repeat them.

Motivation to change the nature of our relationships occurs because we recognize that we are unhappy or that we could be happier. We see that our most intimate relationships are not gratifying and our mistrust of love and relationships has led to substitutes for them that are ultimately unsatisfying. The incentive to be in a relationship or to make the effort to form a more loving or more stable relationship can also come from concerns about aloneness, future illness, or the finiteness of life. Any of these apprehensions may motivate us to reorder our priorities and to search for happiness in an enduring, loving relationship.

It takes courage to look for happiness in what is unfamiliar and uncertain. We need self-discipline to give up our reliance on accustomed pleasures that may have eliminated our need for love. We must make a loving relationship the priority in our life and devote the effort and energy necessary to sustain it. Paradoxically, only after committing to another man and becoming convinced that the relationship with him is essential to one's happiness is it possible to love one's partner for his bad as well as his good qualities and to provide him with the sense of value that will enable him to return an unambivalent, respectful love. It is his love that, over time, will revise the way we experience love and will ultimately change the way we perceive ourselves, others, and the world around us.

Jack

Jack, whom I wrote about in the previous chapter, had parents whose disabilities mandated that he take care of them. Being infirm, they could not provide Jack with much emotional comfort, understanding, or security, so he repressed any desire he had to be close to another man. He had learned early on that his needs usually went unmet. As an adult, he feared that loving another would provide the same frustration, disappointment, and burdens that he had experienced as a child. Since his parents had needed his care and were, in many practical and emotional ways, unable to care for him, he had reason to feel uncared for. Any need he experienced for love as an adult was unbeckoned and unwelcome.

Jack was convinced that he was not lovable, a conviction that had resulted from his not getting the love and the attention he had needed. He had also observed that whatever attention his father had been capable of had been given to his younger siblings. Jack had been a disappointment to his father because he was not as mechanical as his father was and as his father hoped a son would be. His mother had been episodically caring, but she was incapacitated by her disability and later by alcoholism. When she was attentive and affectionate, she was too physical with him for his comfort and too needy to ameliorate his growing mistrust of love.

Therapy had helped Jack to recognize how his early need for security and love had been frustrated by having to take care of disabled parents whose inability to give him the understanding and love he had needed had made him mistrust close relationships. Over time, he became better able to care for and about others with less anger and resentment and without feeling unrealistically burdened. Gradually, he began to feel more lovable and to be loving enough to engage in more intimate, romantic relationships.

After a disappointing relationship that had lasted more than a year, Jack fell in love with Matt, whose capacity for caring, physical demonstrativeness, constancy, and fidelity prevailed over Jack's mistrust, convincing him that he needed Matt's love to make his life better. He was determined to make the effort, the compromises, and the sacrifices that would contribute to a happy relationship.

Although he always found Matt attractive, he had to remind himself that both his partner and the relationship made it worth relinquishing the pleasures of readily available sex. Not diverting his sexual desire, he found, enhanced his need for Matt, made the relationship better, and made his desire for Matt stronger. It took motivation inspired by reflection on his self-interest, as well as considerable self-discipline, to give up the random sex that was so easily available to him. This increased self-discipline and the courage to love despite the hardships of his childhood were by-products of therapy. The therapeutic process had helped to enhance Jack's self-regard enough for him to believe he was worth being loved. Now he could value the effort that was necessary to elicit and nourish this love.

It was Matt's love, however, and not therapy that ultimately revised the way Jack felt about love and altered the way he viewed himself and others. A short while after Matt had moved in, Jack finally completed the work on his apartment that he had delayed for years. He wanted a nice home, he told me, because Matt made him feel that he deserved it and because he wanted a comfortable place to share with his partner.

Ambition had previously eluded Jack because his parents had made him believe that time and attention devoted to any endeavor other than them would injure and deprive them. Nevertheless, a couple of years into his relationship with Matt, Jack, as a result of feeling more deserving and more lovable, asked for and received a promotion, greater recognition, and a higher salary at work. He was also able to enjoy his job more and did not find it quite so oppressively demanding of his time and energy.

He regrets having less time for his friendships, but when he does see his friends, he feels less burdened by their demands, less overwhelmed by their needs, and not as mistrustful of their love and attention as he was before he met Matt. He now feels more love for them. Occasionally, he feels deprived of his previous freedom to pursue sex or to party, and, from time to time, he mourns the loss of these pleasures, but he has never been as content with his life or felt as happy.

Terrence

Terrence came to see me because he found his friendships unsatisfying and was unable to sustain a loving romantic relationship. Like Jack, he had friends, including some whom he cared about a great deal, but he felt detached from them. He had casual sex and short-term relationships, but he never derived much gratification from these either. He viewed himself as a "serial dater" but, at thirty-five, was finding superficial relationships increasingly ungratifying.

His mother had been inhibited in loving her children by her own belief that she was unlovable, which was reinforced by her husband's withdrawal, depression, and unavailability. She had made Terrence her confidant, but he believed that she appreciated him only for the satisfaction he could give her and not for his intrinsic qualities. She wanted him to be well behaved and grown up at an early age, and he attempted to fulfill these expectations. Though he was "special" and knew that he was his mother's favorite, he also felt guilty sharing her confidences about his father and his younger brother.

Early in therapy, Terrence had attributed his father's indifference to Terrence not being a typical boy and to his younger brother being more masculine and athletic than he was. Later, he also recognized that he had used his closeness to his mother to make his father feel unneeded and jealous. Unconsciously, he was certain that his father and his brother had been irreparably harmed and diminished by his special closeness to his mother.

Terrence and his mother shared many interests, but their relationship was sustained by her need for him, as well as by his wish to be her favorite. To please her, he had learned to be deferential, charming, and successful, but nothing he did seemed good enough for her, so he elaborated on his successes and lied about what he believed were his failings or mistakes. By his late adolescence and certainly as an adult, these elaborations and distortions about his accomplishments and failings, which had been necessary to maintain his mother's attention, made him less accepted by peers and contributed to his unhappiness when he started therapy.

Guilt over the harm Terrence believed his mother's devotion to him had inflicted on his father and his brother and the ways he garnered her attention became prominent themes in our work together. He always tried to be interesting but maintained an emotional distance, understandably mistrustful that I could care about him apart from his being smart and entertaining. He attempted to lessen any perceived conflict with me, such as might arise from a scheduling problem, giving me an involved, intricate excuse that was so elaborate, it signaled that he believed he was doing something wrong and was afraid that he would anger me.

He dated occasionally during the first year or two of therapy but inevitably criticized everyone, finding each person deficient in one way or another, losing interest, and then moving on to someone else. He preferred casual, entertaining friends to romantic encounters. However, as he slowly grew more trusting, he became less critical, dated more frequently, and became romantically involved for increasing periods of time. Eventually, he met Mark, who was reliable, undemandingly devoted, and also conflict-avoidant. By then, Terrence felt somewhat more deserving of love and more self-assured because he understood that his guilt stemmed from vanquishing his brother and his father, only to be left with a manipulative, self-involved mother. He had grown to trust me a little more and observed that I, unlike his mother, cared about his well-being apart from his being entertaining, smart, and successful.

I've been able to watch the positive effects Mark has had on Terrence's life over the last six years. Although Terrence has tested Mark from time to time, the consistency of Mark's love has helped to ameliorate Terrence's belief that he was simply instrumental to others and that his value was contingent solely upon the entertainment and the pleasure he provided. Feeling secure in and comforted by this relationship has enabled Terrence to be more discerning of and more honest with friends and to spend time, whenever possible, with those whom he knows and cares about, rather than with people who, like his mother, might use him for their own purposes or whom he could entertain or be entertained by. His increased self-confidence has given him more energy for vocational interests, and he has felt, for the first time, the gratification of "doing something for myself." Mark's love has gradually revised the way Terrence had learned to experience love and relationships.

Jason

Jason, a successful thirty-five-year-old man, came for treatment two years after leaving an unhappy relationship of several years. He was depressed, anxious, and full of self-loathing.

Jason's mother and his father had humiliated him for being effeminate, for his sloppy appearance, and for his indifferent school performance. His father clearly favored his more outgoing, more masculine, and athletic older brother. Jason felt that he had been a disappointment to both parents. In spite of his mother's abusiveness, Jason had admired her intelligence, and their shared interests had made them close. Her approval was important, and separations from her were painful. When he was four or five and she left him, as she frequently did, to attend one of her numerous social functions, he often stood at the window and sobbed uncontrollably. His mother would not stay home or comfort or reassure him at these times, possibly because she believed she had encouraged their close relationship and was responsible for his distress. Leaving her when he went to kindergarten was so traumatic that she had to stay with him in the classroom. The severity of his anxiety suggested that Jason feared being abandoned, a fear that had been caused by his mother's frequent indifference to his needs and her occasional cruelty.

Jason's relationship with his father contributed to his

fear of being abandoned. Jason's father's work frequently took him away from home, and, when in the city, he worked late to escape his wife's demeaning and humiliating comments. Her disdain for her husband and his obvious preference for this patient's older brother caused Jason to believe that he and his father had little in common, a conviction that continued long after his father's death when Jason was about twenty.

Jason had been aware of his attraction to boys since early adolescence, but, concerned about his mother's rejection, he did not seek therapy until he was in his late twenties to cure a depression that he believed was caused by his homosexual inclinations. It was during this treatment that he met Tom, a graduate student who, like his mother, was often cruel, critical, disdainful, and at times as dismissive as his father had been. Only a few months after they moved in together, both men resumed sexual encounters with others and shortly thereafter they stopped having sex with each other. They grew increasingly distant, each pursuing his own vocational and sexual interests, and they eventually separated after about three years. A few years later, Jason started to work with me.

Jason initially complained that I must be repulsed by him and, like his father, was unappreciative of his fine qualities. He was convinced that I preferred my other, more masculine patients to him. He was sarcastic and dismissive and denigrated my efforts to help him; it was only through constant vigilance and restraint that I did not gratify his need for a familiar sought-after criticism and rejection. Over several years of our working together, he cautiously grew more trusting and accepting of my concern and my interest in his being happier. These were the initial steps toward increasing his sense of self-worth.

His perception that relationships could be more loving than those he had known began to change further with the knowledge that he had sought love from men like Tom, who were as dismissive and disrespectful of him as his father had been. As his self-esteem gradually improved, he became increasingly dissatisfied with the quality of men he had been dating and started to appreciate more those men who could care about him.

He was about thirty-eight, good-looking, intelligent, and very successful when he met David, who was a few years younger than he was, through an online dating service. They enjoyed each other sexually and began to spend a considerable amount of time together. After about a year, David moved into Jason's apartment.

David was not as well educated as Jason nor did he have a comparably remunerative job, but he was intelligent, direct, responsive, affectionate, and caring. Jason no longer felt compelled to be with a partner who was familiarly critical, dismissive, or emotionally ungiving. He had fallen in love for the first time with a man who was capable of expressing his love and regard.

Because Jason was now better able to experience himself as lovable, he could be more attentive to David's needs and be more loving and more accepting of the love that David in turn gave him. Jason's ever-increasing self-regard, propelled by David's love, mitigated his need for the casual sexual contacts outside of the relationship that had made him feel less passion and less connected to David. Sex with David became increasingly gratifying, even as it became more familiar and routine, because it was shared pleasure that always made them feel closer to one another.

The manner in which David cared for and about Jason dramatically mitigated Jason's sensitivity to rejection and his corresponding need to reject and criticize others. He found he had less time for his friends, but it was easier to be more caring of them and even of acquaintances who had previously and unfailingly aggravated him. Because he was more self-assured, work was also less burdensome, and because of his greater willingness to take professional risks that might incur criticism, he became increasingly successful. The painful depression that had been caused by his feeling chronically unloved before he met David had disappeared.

A warm adult love and relatedness seem to produce a release of opiatelike chemicals in the brain that is soothing and comforting. Just as loss and abandonment evoke a chemical response that may cause despair or depression, a loving relationship may elicit a physiological response that over time results in a feeling of contentment. Thomas Lewis wrote, "A relationship is a physiological process, as real and as potent as any pill or surgical procedure."

My patients have also discovered that a loving relationship provides them with the self-assurance that enables them to have more energy to devote to work and to the pursuit of new endeavors. They experience more gratification from simple pleasures and have learned to treat others, especially their partners, more honestly, more caringly, and more lovingly. The trust in and commitment to another enable them to experience a better love than they had ever known before.

It is this different experience of love that through its

repetition modifies the neural networks that were formed when we were young children. It is this different experience of love that gives us the ability to change our lives and the lives of others.

Epilogue

The love of another person in an intimate, caring, and sexual relationship, sustained over many years, is the cure for the impoverished self-love of gay men who were hurt in childhood by parental rejection or indifference to their distinctive needs and later traumatized by peer rejection and by a culture that demeans their passion. Gay men who then become mistrustful, fearful, or unaware of their need for love seek happiness without intimacy or intimacy without commitment. They grow habituated to the methods they have used to lessen their need for love: random sex or brief affairs combined with friendships, work, and tasteful surroundings.

Parents' indifference to the feelings of their homosexual children or their outright rejection of these children is caused by the bias that still exists in our society. Despite the gains made over the last ten or twenty years, we still have much to do to achieve equality and acceptance; this includes legalizing same-sex marriages and integrating openly gay men and women into the military. Even when the time does come when society is less ambivalent, it will likely take several generations for parental attitudes to change so that the unique feelings and needs of gay children are valued and not denied.

In the meantime, it will be up to educators and mental health providers to help parents understand how their homosexual children are different from and similar to other children—and how important it is to provide the love, the respect, and the affirmation that will make it possible for them to have healthy self-respect and self-love. Some organizations are currently attempting to do this work, but more must be done until cultural change makes such educational endeavors less urgent.

For the foreseeable future, many if not most gay men will have a hard time believing that they are worth the effort it takes to find a partner or seeing the benefits of loving and being loved by one other person over a long period of time. Only the conviction that love is essential for their happiness and well-being will give them the necessary incentive to express need for a love that they have disavowed. Educators, mental health professionals, religious leaders, and the gay media can all help to provide this conviction by emphasizing that one's ultimate happiness evolves mainly from a committed, loving relationship.

They can also stress the importance of striving for sexual fidelity, which helps gay men to express commitment, maintain passion, and engender trust within their intimate relationships. This can be done without shaming or denigrating the pleasure of experiencing and expressing sexual desire. In an effort to engender self-acceptance and out of an understandable fear of reinforcing shame, the gay community in general and the gay media in particular have expended considerably more time, money, and effort extolling the pleasures of sexual expression than in affirming the happiness that may result from a long-term loving relationship.

There are practical reasons for this emphasis on sex rather than on love: it is easier for a young adult who is in conflict about his sexual orientation to appreciate the pleasure of his sexual desire than to recognize and express his need to love and be loved. Sex is easier to hide from family and friends, and, for the gay media, it is easier to sell. The priority given to sexual expression over love in a misguided effort to help young adults accept themselves has contributed to the difficulty some gay men have incorporating sex into their loving relationships.

I am frequently asked by patients, after they have been with a partner for three or four years and are now becoming dissatisfied or critical, whether they should look for a better boyfriend. Providing there are no glaring problems such as emotional or physical abuse and if both do care about one another, there is a much greater chance of the current boyfriend becoming what they are looking for than there is of finding someone new who will be better. What eventually makes one's partner the best boyfriend possible is a commitment to loving him and a consequent concern about and responsiveness to his needs. This commitment will usually cause him, in turn, to be loving and caring, making it very difficult to find someone new who will be as loving as one's partner of several years.

Many gay men experience boredom after a period of

time with their partners because they are anxious about their own vulnerability, neediness, and dependency. The continuing effort it takes to make a relationship as loving as it can possibly be may be frightening, but it should not be boring.

Most gay men who have struggled since childhood and are aware that they have suffered because they were different from others have within themselves the capacity to find partners and the courage and the tenacity to sustain loving bonds. When they choose to take these risks, their lives will be happier.

Loving another man and being loved by him helps a gay man become a better and more compassionate human being.

Notes

1. The Problem of Romantic Love

The epigraph to this chapter is drawn from Franz Rosenzweig, *The Star of Redemption*, trans. William Hallo (Notre Dame: University of Notre Dame Press, 1985), p. 179.

9 *I do not limit the concept* I am indebted to Irving Singer for his discussion of romantic love in the third volume of his trilogy *The Nature of Love* (Chicago and London: University of Chicago Press, 1987). He divides romantic love into three stages: falling in love, being in love, and staying in love, with "being in love" the intermediate stage of bond creation. This division into three stages does help to define and describe the nature of love, but since patients usually seek help because they have a problem falling in love or staying in love, I discuss the difficulties that arise in the creation of an enduring bond between lovers as a problem with "staying in love."

10 *"inhibited in their aims"* Sigmund Freud, *Group Psychology and the Analysis of the Ego*, SE18 (London: Hogarth Press, 1921), p. 139.

11 *The absence of this structure* See Evan Wolfson, *Why Marriage Matters* (New York: Simon and Schuster, 2004).

11 *many gay men lack self-love* In writing about the difficulty gay men have with romantic love, I am not reverting to the model of traditional orthodox psychoanalytic practitioners who maintained that homosexuals, because of their "perverse" sexuality, were ipso facto unable to love. Until the mid-1980s, most psychoanalysts believed that it was impossible for homosexuals to form stable, sustained, loving

attachments because this was the domain of only relatively "normal" people: "Incapacity to love is of course a common characteristic of all the (homosexual) patients we have observed, which confirms if it be necessary, the immaturity of their personality." S. Nacht, R. Diatkine, and J. Fabreau, "The Ego in Perverse Relationships" (*International Journal of Psychoanalysis* 37 [1956]: 404–13). Or, "From the point of view of object relations, normal sexuality is characterized by true object cathexis in which the partner matters as an individual, is not used as a means to an end, is highly cathected and is valued. . . . The so called passionate love relationships between perverts lack these unique characteristics." G. Devereaux (*Journal of the American Psychoanalytic Association* 2 [1954]). For a scholarly discussion of the psychoanalytic view of homosexuality from its inception until 1983, see Kenneth Lewes, *The Psychoanalytic Theory of Male Homosexuality* (New York: Simon and Schuster, 1988).

12   *heterosexual men and gay men alike*   See Stephen A. Mitchell, *Can Love Last?* (New York: W. W. Norton & Company, 2002).

13   *I am not confident that this freedom*   Such ideas are espoused, among others, by Richard D. Mohr, *Gay Ideas: Outing and Other Controversies* (Boston: Beacon Press, 1992), p. 201, and Dennis Altman, *The Homosexuality of America* (Boston: Beacon Press, 1982), chapter 6.

13   *artistic, civic, and financial contributions*   See David Nimmons, *The Soul beneath the Skin: The Unseen Hearts and Habits of Gay Men* (New York: St. Martin's Press, 2002), p. 5.

15   *risky sexual behavior is again rising*   For the relationship between the rise in the use of crystal methamphetamine and HIV, see the articles "H.I.V. Infections Continue to Rise" (*New York Times*, November 27, 2003), Section A, page 28; "The Beast in the Bathhouse" (*New York Times*, January 12, 2004), Section B, page 1; and "Higher Risk" (*The New Yorker* [May 23, 2005]): 38–45.

15   *Outside of metropolitan areas*   The authors of a large, ethnically diverse study of gay men and women in communities of varying sizes around the Bay Area did also find that gay men "do not value a long-term relationship" and that their relationships were "relatively unstable." They observed that "close-coupled" partners who turn to each other rather than to outsiders for sexual and interpersonal satisfactions tended to have "superior adjustment" related to their sexual orientation and to be "more exuberant than the average respondent." See Alan P. Bell and Martin S. Weinberg, *Homosexualities: A Study of Diversity among Men and*

Women (New York: Simon and Schuster, 1978), pp. 85–102, 219–220.

16 *"No one kind of love"* Irving Singer, op. cit., volume 3, p. 436.

16 *"In the business of acquiring immortality* Plato, *Symposium*, translated by Robin Waterfield (Oxford and New York: Oxford University Press, 1994), p. 56, line 212b.

2. Why Is It Difficult to Need Love?

The epigraph to this chapter is drawn from Plato, *Symposium*, op. cit., p. 45, line 204a.

19 *This premature birth results in* See Willard Gaylin, *Rediscovering Love* (New York: Penguin Books, 1986), p. 33.

20 *imprinted memories of our early relatedness* Thomas Lewis, Fari Amini, and Richard Lannon, *A General Theory of Love* (New York: Random House, 2000), chapter 4.

21 *the lack of human interaction* See René A. Spitz, "Hospitalism: An Inquiry into the Genesis of Psychiatric Conditions in Early Childhood" (*Psychoanalytic Study of the Child* I [1945]): 53–74.

21 *John Bowlby* For a review of Bowlby's work, Mary Ainsworth's, and the work of other pioneers who demonstrated how early attachments affect the capacity for adult relationships, see Robert Karen, *Becoming Attached: First Relationships and How They Shape Our Capacity to Love* (New York and Oxford: Oxford University Press, 1998).

21 *undermine the child's self-esteem* See Alice Miller, *Prisoners of Childhood* (New York: Basic Books, 1981).

24 *characteristics that are more often associated with girls* See Richard Green, *The Sissy Boy Syndrome and the Development of Homosexuality* (New Haven and London: Yale University Press, 1987). For a review of the studies on gender atypicality and homosexual boys, see Simon LeVay, *Queer Science: The Use and Abuse of Research in Homosexuality* (Cambridge and London: MIT Press, 1996). Also see Richard C. Friedman and Jennifer I. Downey, *Sexual Orientation and Psychoanalysis* (New York: Columbia University Press, 2002), chapter 2. For a phenomenological view of homosexual boyhood, see Ken Corbett, "Homosexual Boyhood: Notes on Girly Boys" (*Gender and Psychoanalysis* 1 no. 4 [1996]): 429–462. The hypothesis that I believe best explains the concordance between childhood gender atypicality and adult homosexuality is that espoused by Simon LeVay (op. cit., p. 160): "homosexuality is part of a package of sex transposed traits."

25   *lose touch with the frustrated needs*   I elaborate on this high emotional cost of repudiating feminine traits and especially emotional
expressiveness in my article "Gender in Homosexual Boys: Some
Developmental and Clinical Considerations" (*Psychiatry* 62 [1999]):
187–194.

30   *"You may live in two places"*   Daniel Mendelsohn, *The Elusive
Embrace* (New York: Alfred A. Knopf, 1999), p. 205.

31   *"It has been some years"*   Quoted in my book *Becoming Gay: The
Journey to Self-Acceptance* (New York: Pantheon Books, 1996), p. 95. In
chapter 4, I discuss "The Dilemma of Heterosexually Married Homosexual Men."

31   *"In almost every regard"*   Andrew Sullivan, *Love Undetectable*
(New York: Alfred A. Knopf, 1998), p. 202.

34   *"The mastery of the art"*   Erich Fromm, *The Art of Loving* (New
York: Perennial Library Edition, 1956), p. 5.

3. Love and Sex in Adult Gay Relationships

The epigraph to this chapter is drawn from Larry Kramer, *Faggots*
(New York: Warner Books, 1978), p. 44.

38   *Within the first two or three years*   In one study of 156 gay couples, none of the couples together more than five years were sexually
exclusive with each other. See David P. McWhirter and Andrew Mattison, *The Male Couple* (Englewood Cliffs, N.J.: Prentice-Hall, 1984), p.
285.

38   *Not only gay men*   In his survey of heterosexual couples, Kinsey
found that 26 percent of wives and 50 percent of husbands had had
extramarital sexual relations at least once during their marriages. See
Alfred Kinsey, Wardell Pomeroy, and Clyde Martin, *Sexual Behavior in
the Human Female* (Philadelphia: W. B. Saunders, 1953). A *Playboy* mag-
azine survey in 1983 that elicited 100,000 responses from five million
readers found that 34 percent of women and 45 percent of men had had
extramarital sex (James R. Peterson, *Playboy* 30, no. 3: 90ff). In *The
Janus Report on Sexual Behavior*, S. S. Janus and D. Z. Janus (1993)
report that 26 percent of women and 35 percent of men had extramarital sex. These findings all suggest that approximately 25 percent of
women and 50 percent of men have sex outside of their marriages at
least once. See Shirley P. Glass, *Not "Just Friends"* (New York: Free
Press, 2003), p. 387.

38   *"where they love, they do not desire"*   Sigmund Freud, "On the

Universal Tendency to Debasement in the Sphere of Love" (1912), S.E. 11, p. 183.

38 *"completely normal attitude in love"* Sigmund Freud, op. cit., p. 180.

39 *"I see no marriages"* From "On Some Verses of Virgil," *The Complete Essays of Montaigne*, translated by Donald M. Frame (New York: Anchor Books, 1960), volume 3, p. 69. Quoted by Irving Singer in *The Nature of Love*, op. cit., volume 2, p. 258.

39 *Bertrand Russell* Discussed by Irving Singer, *The Nature of Love*, op cit., volume 3, p. 6.

39 *sex with others* David McWhirter and Andrew Mattison, *The Male Couple*, pp. 61–65.

39 *"neither partner is prepared to subordinate"* Dennis Altman, *The Homosexualization of America* (New York: St Martin's Press, 1982), p. 186.

39 *"fuck buddies, communal homes"* David Nimmons, *The Soul beneath the Skin: The Unseen Hearts and Habits of Gay Men*, op. cit., pp. 7–8.

40 *Where monogamy has evolved* See E. O. Wilson, *Sociobiology: The New Synthesis* (Boston: Harvard University Press, 1976), pp. 330–332.

42 *Dennis Altman's view* See Dennis Altman, op. cit., p. 189.

42 *making the vulnerability itself exciting* Discussed by Stephen Mitchell, *Can Love Last?* op. cit., pp. 39–49.

45 *This painful emotion* See E. O. Wilson, op. cit., pp. 242–243.

46 *"When one is . . . able"* Richard Mohr, op. cit., p. 200.

46 *"We should put an end"* Bruce Voeller, an early organizer of the National Gay Task Force, quoted by Dennis Altman in *The Homosexualization of America*, op. cit., p. 176.

46 *"the single most important"* David McWhirter and Andrew Mattison, *The Male Couple*, op. cit., p. 256.

51 *Homosexual boys* Discussed by R. Blanchard, J. G. McConkey, V. Roper, and B. Steiner, "Measuring Physical Aggressiveness in Heterosexual, Homosexual, and Transsexual Males" (*Archives of Sexual Behavior* 12 [1985]): 511–524. Also see Richard Green, *The Sissy Boy Syndrome* (New Haven: Yale University Press, 1987).

52   *David*   This case is included in the chapter on "Developing a
sitive Gay Identity with HIV or AIDS," in my book *Becoming Gay:*
Journey to Self-Acceptance, op. cit., pp. 119–137.

alling in Love

epigraph to this chapter is drawn from Michel de Montaigne, "On
dship," in *Essays*, trans. J. M Cohen (London: Penguin Books, 1958),
Montaigne was writing about his first meeting with a friend who
few years later. We have no reason to assume that he and his friend
xual relationship. Yet, because Montaigne describes so beautifully
on, idealization, longing, and fusion that occur when one falls in
do have reason to assume that he fell in love with his friend.

"*It was their very essence*"   Plato, *Symposium*, op. cit, line 191b,

'*The deepest need*"   Erich Fromm, *The Art of Loving* (New
rper & Row, Perennial Library Edition, 1989), pp. 9–10.

Deprivation in infancy   Otto Kernberg suggests that depriva-
neglect in the earliest developmental stages are solely respon-
ne's inability to fall in love. See his article "Barrier to Falling
ining in Love" (*Journal of the American Psychoanalytic Associa-*
. 3 [1974]): 486–515.

; in Love

iph to this chapter is drawn from Erich Fromm, *The Art of*
cit., p. 51.

netimes a mother   The role of mothers in the childhood of
l boys is discussed by Scott Goldsmith in his article "Oedi-
tes? Homosexual Men, Their Mothers, and Other Women
Journal of the American Psychoanalytic Association 49, no. 4
59–87. Also see his earlier article "Oedipus or Orestes?
ender Identity Development in Homosexual Men" (*Psycho-*
iry 15 [1995]): 112–24.

freedoms that they lose"   Irving Singer, op. cit., volume 3,

uperficial attributes   Irving Singer calls the type of love in
on defines his own value by such superficial attributes of
raisive" love. All love, he writes, includes both appraisive-
owal, but appraisive love belongs more to the stage of
, and bestowal, to staying in love. "Valuation through

appraisal belongs to our appetitive being, which causes us to appropriate objects, including people, for the sake of our own gratification. But love implies that we want, and care about, the welfare of the beloved." *The Nature of Love*, op. cit., volume 3, p. 393.

6. How Therapy Works

The epigraph to this chapter is drawn from Erich Fromm, *The Heart of Man* (New York: Harper & Row, 1964), p. 150.

105 *it is usually beneficial* I wrote about this issue in my book *Becoming Gay: The Journal to Self-Acceptance*, op. cit., chapter 2, on "The Gay Therapist."

105 *the transference will be unaffected* There are two important exceptions to the transference being unaffected by knowledge of a therapist's sexual orientation. When a gay patient is ambivalent about his sexuality and his self-regard has been so injured that he dislikes gay men and wants to be heterosexual, or when a gay man feels sexually threatened by a therapist who is gay because he was sexually abused as a child, then antipathy to a gay therapist is often so immediate and so powerful that it is not amenable to understanding. These patients, I believe, are better off being treated by a thoughtful, caring, straight therapist. Though powerful negative feelings are likely to occur with that therapist as well, they are usually manifested later on in treatment when the patient is better able to understand them.

106 *this loving attitude* See Hans Loewald, "On the Therapeutic Action of Psychoanalysis" (*International Journal of Psychoanalysis* 41 [1960]): 16–33.

107 *"on the surgeon"* Sigmund Freud, "Recommendations to the Physician Practicing Psychoanalysis" (Standard Edition, volume 12, 1912), p. 115; *"nothing but what is shown,"* ibid., page 118.

108 *Ferenczi* See Sandor Lorand, "Sandor Ferenczi," in *Psychoanalytic Pioneers*, edited by Franz Alexander, Samuel Eisenstein, and Martin Grotjahn (New York: Basic Books, 1966), pages 14–35. And also see Sandor Ferenczi, "The Further Development of an Active Therapy," in *Further Contributions to the Theory and Technique of Psychoanalysis* (Great Britain: Hogarth Press, 1969), pp. 198–217.

108 *"the essence of the therapeutic process"* Franz Alexander, *The Scope of Psychoanalysis* (New York: Basic Books, 1961), p. 327.

109 *"serves as a focal point"* "On the Therapeutic Action of Psychoanalysis," op. cit., p. 32.

110   *"Anomalous love"*   Thomas Lewis, Fari Amini, and Richard Lannon, *A General Theory of Love* (New York: Random House, 2000), p. 160.

7. The Therapeutic Power of Love

The epigraph to this chapter is drawn from Franz Rosenzweig, *The Star of Redemption*, op. cit., p. 424.

127   *"A relationship is a physiological process"*   Thomas Lewis et al., *A General Theory of Love*, op. cit., p. 81. In chapter 4, the authors discuss the neurophysiology of separation and of love and attachment.

Epilogue

132   *Some organizations*   The Parents and Friends of Lesbians and Gays (P-Flag) provides education and support for the parents of gays and lesbians. The Out-Reach Program for Children with Gender-Variant Behavior and Their Families (202-884-2504), based in Washington, D.C., educates parents about the gender-atypical traits of their gay and lesbian children and offers support to them and their children. To improve the lives of adolescents, GLISEN provides education and support for teenagers, their friends, and their teachers in gay-straight alliances within schools.

133   *The priority given*   Gabriel Rotello has written that the gay community should encourage the "connections between sex and intimacy . . . and end the pervasive belief that those who are among the most extreme fringes of gay sexual life are somehow the most liberated and the most gay." *Sexual Ecology* (New York: Dutton, 1997), p. 244.

Index